T0193136

The Little Book of
BIG LOVE
from
HEAVEN

STEPHANIE LYNN FUNK

BALBOA.
PRESS
A DIVISION OF HAY HOUSE

Balboa Press books may be ordered through booksellers or by contacting:

Balboa Press
A Division of Hay House
1663 Liberty Drive
Bloomington, IN 47403
www.balboapress.com
1 (877) 407-4847

Print information available on the last page.

ISBN: 978-1-9822-0865-3 (sc)
ISBN: 978-1-9822-0866-0 (e)

Balboa Press rev. date: 07/25/2018

My Heartfelt Thank You To:

Our Heavenly Father ~ I would not be writing this book if it were not for a loving Heavenly Father. His awesome love shown to me in ways I could not imagine started my writing the series of loving events in a journal. I had no idea that I would be sharing them later. His promptings and nudging convinced me that I was to share this story of His love.

My husband and best friend for 25 years, Pete ~ He showed me a new way of love, support and comfort in his spiritual life that I did not want to forget.

Lisa Vyas of Balboa Press ~ Lisa patiently waited for me to finish the book. She is a great listener and gave me guidance and confidence throughout this process. She also introduced me to the Author Learning Center where I gained valuable advice and knowledge on writing a book.

To Kathryn ~ She reviewed my manuscript and gave me constructive suggestions for improving my story.

To my good friends, Nira and Gerri, for their patience in listening to all my heavenly encounters over the years.

The online mentors who don't know that I exist but graciously gave video trainings that gave me the confidence I needed to push forward on this book.

Contents

2015 ~ More Decisions with Help and Humor

2016 ~ Messages

2017 ~ Dreams

Introductory Comments and Thoughts

Have you ever had an experience or event in your life that was hard to explain or understand because it seemed impossible, but it left a deep impression on you? Did it ever occur to you that this might be heaven giving you a hug? I really never thought about being hugged from heaven but that started changing in 2012.

I am a hugger. I love hugs. There has been a lot of documentation regarding our need for frequent hugs suggesting that it is good for our physical and mental health. Hugs make us feel good. I was always able to get my many daily hugs from my best hugging friend, my husband, until he passed away in 2013. I didn't realize how much those regular hugs meant to me.

I grew up knowing God and knowing that I was God's child. God and heaven were real in theory and knowledge for me, but it seemed more "out there" than right here and now. Although I had unexplainable events happen in my life, I hadn't connected the dots of their importance in my relationship with God and heaven.

An example of one such unexplainable incident occurred in 1993. At the time I did not understand this event. My husband and I were traveling to northern Arizona for a road race. We were runners and ran races most weekends. He was driving and I was reading a book. I heard a voice say, "Lynn look up" and again only louder, "Lynn look up" and again but this time yelling at me, "Lynn look up." I threw the book up in the air and looked up out the front windshield.

My husband was passing a semi-truck and there was a car coming towards us. I screamed, "Pete, Pete" and he seemed to realize what was happening. He floored the accelerator on our truck, as there wasn't time to pull back. At the same time the semi driver also realized what was happening and he put on his brakes to make it easier for our truck to quickly get in front. The vehicle coming at us went off the road. No one was hurt. We were shaken, but I was more shaken by the voice that yelled at me. It was as if there was another person in the truck with us.

I shared with my husband about the voice. It seemed like minutes but it was all in split seconds. My husband kind of remembered my throwing the book and my screaming his name. He was not asleep but evidently in some sort of trance. That voice and the event stayed with me. I have questioned why and how many times, as I really did not fully understand. This wasn't the first or last of these types of events. I just hadn't connected them necessarily to God and/or to heaven.

In 2013 right after my husband passed away, I realized that I was having more of these most unusual, hard-to-explain loving events happening. They had actually been happening since the summer of 2012, but now I didn't want to forget the love I realized I was receiving. In the summer of 2013 I started writing journal entries but went back to the beautiful signs I started receiving in 2012. I wrote in a spiral notebook that my husband had written some last instructional notes for me. I had this spiral notebook in my desk and it seemed the appropriate place to write these journal entries. I had no idea when I started writing these loving events that there would be so many to write about and that I would be nudged years later to share them.

The nudging from God started in the summer of 2017. I felt He was asking me to share my spiritual journey with others. I was not comfortable with the sharing or with the writing, but God will do whatever it takes to get your attention. He reminded me that this was His book about His love and it really was His story. I was merely the recipient of His heavenly hugs and love through this journey.

I did ask that if He really wanted me to write, could He please guide me because I had no clue how to get started. Boy, did He show me. Facebook ads regarding writing a book were appearing and I received emails stating, "Have you considered writing a book?" Doors started opening. I have to smile because God does have a sense of humor.

Since the summer of 2017 and God's initial promptings, I have been awakened at night and reminded of other past events, which made an impact on me, but I hadn't thought about in a long time. I would be told to go write them down. I would get up and go write a sticky note to remind me in the morning. One night I had written one note, got back in bed and God reminded me of another event, so I got back up and wrote another sticky note. As I was heading back to bed, I asked God if He had more for me to remember could he remind me before I got back in bed. That seemed to be all for that night. All of this was happening after the initial nudging to write this book in the summer of 2017.

As I was following God's prompting to write, and I was pulling all these individual events together for this book, I started to see an amazing pattern of heavenly love that has been showered on my life. It was as if each individual event was a loving thread when woven together with all the other loving events created a beautiful tapestry of heavenly love and hugs wrapped around me. I had been and always was hugged by heaven; I just had not connected the dots.

This book is not one story but a collection of loving events on my journey to understanding heaven in a new light. My hope in sharing my journey is that others will see the pattern of heaven's love and hugs in my life events and see a reflection of heaven's love and hugs in their own life journey.

2012

Spiritual Awakening

God Hugs
Summer 2012

Sometime in the summer of 2012 I started having experiences that were so wonderful and so awesome that I didn't want them to go away. On a couple of occasions I wanted to go with whatever loving presence had just passed through me. These experiences were different than anything I had ever experienced before.

My life was happy and filled with love. I had a wonderful, fun husband of almost twenty-five years, and we were doing what we believed God wanted us to do. We were sharing our talents and gifts. We had loving families. I couldn't ask for more. I was once asked if my husband, Pete, and I ever argued. In all honesty, Pete and I NEVER argued.... EVER! This wasn't our first marriage, and we never dreamed we would marry again, so we entered the marriage wanting it to work. We were not fighters. We had differences of opinion, but possibly because we were long-distance runners, we had lots of time to work out the differences while we were running all those miles. Early in our marriage, we learned a concept of "seeking first to understand another before being understood." That worked for us when it came to differences.

I honestly don't know when these events, I am about to share, started in the summer of 2012. They did not occur with any regularity or at any specific time. It was very random. One instance, which was one of the strongest, happened while I was waiting for a streetlight to change. I was watching the pansies along the median dancing in the wind. All of a sudden I had this feeling of immense love passing through from the right side of my body to the left, and I smelled the freshest smell I have ever smelled. The smell was like after a rain; that clean fresh smell but more intense. Every time I had one of these events, they only lasted a few seconds, but in all cases, I wanted to go with whatever or whoever was there. I had never felt this kind of love before. It was complete, and I thought I had the best love in my physical life. This was just so different, and I didn't know why I was having these experiences.

I shared these encounters with my husband, Pete, and started calling them my "God Hugs." I didn't know what else to call them. It just felt like I had been hugged by heaven.

During the summer of 2012, I also had two other unusual types of encounters. Both were in my home office.

My mother-in-law's old dresser had a swivel mirror, and the dresser and mirror were in the front left corner of my office. The mirror was positioned so that I could see if someone approached the door to my office. My desk faced the windows of my office, and the door to my office was at my back. Pete loved sneaking up on me while I was working, so the mirror helped me see when he was approaching.

That summer I would be working and sense that I just saw someone in the mirror. I would turn around and there was no one there, but I had a strong sensation that someone was in the room with me. This happened a lot. I was not afraid because I felt love. I just didn't understand why.

I also had a ceiling fan with a light kit just above my desk. The light kit was one that did not wobble. I couldn't handle wobbly lights as they made me dizzy. We had finally found a ceiling fan that had a circular fluorescent light that did not wobble. It was great lighting for over my desk. On occasions that summer it would be as if a cloud had just passed over the light. It did not flicker; it was like cloud movement where it gets a little darker for the time it takes a cloud to pass. I would look up and see nothing, but I sensed I was not alone. I didn't know why this was happening at the time. I only felt love.

In November 2012, my husband and best hugging friend of 25 years was diagnosed with stage 4-lung cancer that had already spread to each lung, his liver, spine, and brain. We were devastated because he did not have any symptoms of such a dreadful disease. He was actively working. We were still running. He had no cough and no shortness of breath. We were sure it was a mistake. It wasn't; he lost his battle with cancer on June 4, 2013.

Looking back, I believe the "God Hugs" I started experiencing the summer of 2012 were to prepare me for the life-altering journey that Pete and I would be going through in the winter of 2012 until his passing in 2013. Throughout that difficult time period, I received many "God Hugs" and had other loving heavenly encounters, which I share in this book.

The joy and the immense love I felt through these encounters helped me stay strong for Pete. God was always "hugging" me and somehow I think He was "hugging" Pete too.

Someone Else In Control
Summer 2012

I separated this event out from the other summer of 2012 events because this one was so different. Sometimes it is hard to explain something that just shouldn't happen, but does and makes you wonder "how" it happened.

Lunchtime was "date" time for Pete and I. Whether we ate at home or out, we enjoyed this time together. One day in the summer of 2012 we met at a restaurant located in the community where we lived. We were finished with lunch, and my husband's work was done for the day so he was going to head home. I was going home to pick up materials for my afternoon appointments.

We were driving on Clearview Boulevard, which has two lanes of traffic for each direction with a median in between the opposing traffic. I was about a half block in front of Pete. At the intersection of Clearview Boulevard and Gold Canyon Drive there was a 4-way stop sign.

I had stopped at the stop sign, and then the next thing I knew I was on the opposite side of the median in the middle of the lanes going the opposite direction. My car was about four to five car lengths from the intersection. A community landscaper turned and looked at me as I whirled my little Toyota Yaris around. I came back to the intersection, but now

I was facing the direction I just came from. On the other side at the intersection at the stop sign was my husband just starring at me. He shrugged his shoulders and put his hands up in the air. When Pete didn't understand something, especially if it was unusual, he would shrug his shoulders and put his hands up in the air as if to say, "What was that?" I just shrugged my shoulders with my hands up in the air, because I had no idea what had just happened.

He went through the intersection, and then I made a U-turn and followed him home. When we got home, he got out of his car and he said to me, "I'm not even going to ask you how you did that. It was like I blinked my eyes and you were at the intersection, and then you were on the other side." I looked at him and said, "Someone else was in control." I didn't know what else to say because I really did not understand what had just happened.

I asked him if he saw any other cars in the intersection, which could have triggered the event. He said there were no other cars. It was just a blink of the eyes and I was transformed from one place to another. I could tell by the landscaper's eyes that he was also dumbfounded by my appearance on that side of the median at that spot. I, too, was just as dumbfounded. I had no idea how I got there or why.

To this day I am not sure why that event happened. I have wondered if God, knowing what was before us, needed to show both my husband I that He was with us and in control of all situations.

In November 2012 when Pete was diagnosed with Stage 4 lung cancer, he seemed to know that God was in control and was with him. Did this summer of 2012 event trigger that? I don't honestly know. During Pete's battle with cancer he taped Bible quotes to his desk that referenced God's control. Pete always said that the outcome didn't matter. It would be a win-win either way.

2013

New Journey

Pete's Visitors
Spring 2013

The spring of 2013 was very difficult for my husband, Pete. Chemotherapy had not helped reduce the tumors, but had physically brought him to his knees. It was at this time that I would find him up during the middle of the night. He would be in his office. He was having nightmares and could only get rid of them by getting up for a little while.

The phenomenon I am about to share is particularly difficult to write, because I still don't understand what I witnessed, but I will share it in the event that others may have had similar experiences. I was never afraid and only felt love.

One night during the last few months of Pete's life I was awakened, and when I looked over at my husband's bed, there was someone sitting on the edge of his bed looking at him. It looked like my husband's profile in a shadowy like form, but my husband was in bed asleep. This shadowy form looked at my husband and then got up from the bed just as my husband would do and moved towards the bathroom door. I say moved because it was not walking, but just seemed to flow to the doorway of the bathroom. It then stopped, looked around and continued moving into the bathroom out of my sight.

The first night this happened, I did not want to move. I was sure I was dreaming, but I felt very awake. I did not want to go back to sleep hoping to see if what I saw would come back, but I did fall back to sleep. The next morning I remembered this vision or dream clearly.

The same phenomenon happened a number of times from the spring of 2013 until my husband's death. It was always the same. I either woke up when the shadowy form was sitting on his bed, or standing in the doorway to the bathroom, or moving from one point to another. It was eerie because the profile and getting up from the bed was so much like my husband, but my husband would always be in bed.

On the nights that I witnessed these encounters, my husband did not have nightmares. I was not afraid and when I kept witnessing these encounters, I somehow felt that whatever I was seeing was there to comfort Pete. I did not share these encounters though with my husband because of his nightmares.

Pete's Visions
June 2-3, 2013

On Saturday, June 1, 2013, Pete had some special friends stop by to visit. It was a beautiful visit. He was alert and very talkative. After about two hours, Pete was starting to get weary. After his visitors left, he asked to go to bed. He told me that Saturday evening that he was ready to go home, meaning heaven. He never left his bed.

Pete's three girls were wonderful. They were with us almost every day the last couple weeks of his life. One stepdaughter and her long-term partner spent the last few nights of his life with us.

That Saturday about 10 pm, I said goodnight to our stepdaughter and her partner. I went into our bedroom and had just gotten into bed, when I heard a crash that seemed to be in our bedroom. However, Pete was in his bed and there was no one else in the room or in the adjoining bathroom. I guessed that the crash might have come from the living room where the kids were spending the night on the couches. I didn't pursue it further.

On Sunday morning, June 2, 2013, I heard my husband stirring in bed and went into him. At this point, he was not able to get up unassisted. When I entered our bedroom, he was looking up to the front right upper corner of the room.

His eyes were open and they were really bright. I sat on the edge of the bed as he looked at the corner of the room.

He finally turned and looked at me, but it was different. It appeared as if he was looking through me not really at me. He said, "The plans have changed. Heaven isn't like this." I made a comment that I knew heaven wasn't like this and wanted to know more, but at that point he indicated that he needed to go to the bathroom. That required help, as he could no longer get up on his own. It required someone on each side of him to assist him.

I called our stepdaughter and her partner into our bedroom to help. As they were trying to get him up from the bed, he was trying to tell them about heaven, and they were trying to tell me that he could no longer shuffle. That meant taking care of his needs in another way.

I knew Pete was mentally still very lucid. Up to this point he had refused pain meds. He still had his wit and humor. He said a comical "Pete-ism," as his younger stepdaughter called them. I had just reminded him of the plan we needed to take to assist him with his needs when he could no longer take care of them himself. At this point I told him I needed his stepdaughter and partner's help with this task, and for preparing his bed for his future needs. That's when he said one of his Pete-ism's, only as Pete could say them, "As long as they don't point and laugh." I sighed and said, "No one is going to point and laugh, honey." He then slipped back into a coma-like state. I was not able to get anything more about heaven from him. He had been slipping in and out of consciousness since his Saturday afternoon visitors left.

Later that Sunday morning when I went to take a shower, I found on our master bedroom closet floor two heavy-duty plastic hangers that had Pete's cargo shorts on them. The necks of both of the hangers were broken. It looked liked the two hangers had been violently pulled off the closet rack. That had to be the noise I heard Saturday night. But how and why?

I picked up the hangers and the necks and laid them on a dresser that was in the closet. I was puzzled. I later showed one of the daughters and asked her what she thought. She too was puzzled. To this day, I still don't know how this occurred. It might make sense if it were one broken hanger, but two? Cargo shorts were Pete's favorite shorts.

On Monday morning, June 3, 2013, I was making tea and I heard Pete rustling in bed. I went to see what he needed. He had not talked since Sunday morning. He was again looking at the same front right corner of the room at the ceiling area. I sat on the edge of the bed and looked and waited. He finally looked at me, and again he was looking through me and not at me. He said, "Where Am I?" I told him he was home. He said, "Oh, I thought I went to heaven this morning." I wanted more, but he again slipped into a coma-like state. Those were the last words I heard from him until about 5:30 that evening.

Around 5 pm on Monday, June 3, 2013, Pete's youngest daughter was holding his hand on one side of the bed, and I was holding his other hand on the other side of the bed. As she was talking to him, tears were rolling down his cheeks. I knew this was agony for her. Pete was her step-dad and raised her from the time she was three years old.

She was now about 45 with two high school boys of her own. She considered Pete her dad and always told him and everyone else that Pete was dad. She was thanking him for all he had taught her. I told her that he was hearing her; he just could not respond. After she left, I was holding his hand and thanking him for his girls and just talking to him in general. I didn't expect anything from him at this point, but I hoped he could hear me. All of a sudden he opened his eyes and looked at me and said, "I Love You." Then he fell back into a coma-like state. I don't remember all that I said to him because I could no longer hold back my tears.

Those were his last words, but oh so precious. They were music to my ears and heart. I say that because early in our relationship Pete felt the words, "I love you" were over used and then were meaningless. He felt loving actions spoke louder than those three words. For me those words were music to my ears and heart and I told him that, but I didn't want him to use those words if it didn't feel right for him. During our early relationship, I made a small sign on a block of wood about the words "I love you" and what they meant to me. He had that block of wood on his desk. As our years together rolled on, he said and wrote the words more frequently, and I knew that when they were said or written, it was from his heart. So his last words, when I thought there were no more, were so precious to me and helped sustain me through the days and months to follow.

Monday night was difficult for him, and for those of us with him. Tuesday, June 4, 2013, around 1:55 in the morning, Pete made it home to heaven. I believe the visions of heaven Pete had the two mornings before he passed away were hugs from heaven to prepare him for his journey to his heavenly home.

The Roadrunners
June 2013

Lunch was always "our date." We almost always ate lunch together whether at home or out. Our table at home was situated so that I sat looking outside to the backyard and he sat across from me with his back to the backyard. It was the first day of my eating alone at home after my husband's passing away.

I looked across the table and of course he wasn't there, and I started crying. All of a sudden there was a roadrunner at the back patio door with its head cocked looking in through the sliding glass door.

I jumped up out of my chair and started talking as if my husband was present saying, "Pete look, a roadrunner. Look, a roadrunner." I continued babbling saying, "We have lived here 12 years and have never seen a roadrunner." By that time the roadrunner was long gone, but I wasn't crying anymore. I just kept talking, more to myself, about seeing the roadrunner.

A couple of days later I am sitting at the table trying to eat lunch, and I am crying. I looked up and there was a roadrunner at the back patio door again! I could not believe I was seeing a second roadrunner, and at the back patio door. This time though I heard the words, "Lynn we're roadrunners, we've even got the jackets." I was so overjoyed that I was now on my feet and dancing around saying, "I got it. I got it." I wasn't crying anymore. I was filled with joy. I was starting to understand something beautiful was happening.

Pete and I were roadrunners, and we were members of an Arizona roadrunners club. We had these paper-thin jackets that were white with blue runners and had the Arizona roadrunners club logo on them. When we lived in North Phoenix, we ran out in the desert and would often see roadrunners. They fascinated us. After we moved further west into our new senior community, we had not seen any roadrunners. So a roadrunner sighting and two of them at the back patio door was definitely unusual.

It didn't end there. Within the same week I was opening the garage door and there was a roadrunner on the driveway of the home across the street! It stopped, cocked its head at me, and then it was gone. That was my third roadrunner sighting in less than a week after not seeing roadrunners in the 12 years we had lived in that community. I can only say that I felt comfort, that God was "hugging" me. When things happen in threes, they are significant for me. These roadrunner sightings happened between Pete's passing and his celebration of life service; about a two-week time span.

It was around this time that I started journaling. I didn't want to forget these beautiful expressions of love.

Pete and his Arizona Roadrunner Jacket

Strange Phone Call
June 2013

Pete worked for AT&T for almost 45 years and had learned many of the industrial trades such as: electricity, electronics, plumbing, heating and cooling, in addition to everything about telephone service. After retirement from AT&T he became a certified home inspector. We ended up closing the business after Pete had an accident at home. A lung contusion from the accident made it difficult for him to perform certain home inspector functions. He ended up needing surgery to repair the area of the lung contusion.

After we closed the business and Pete had healed from the accident, we moved to a senior community. It wasn't long and Pete was restless. He went to work for a fairly large church as Maintenance and Security and worked for another organization doing handyman work and installing lifeline telephone alert systems. He was gifted in all the trades but especially with electronics, electricity and telephone service.

Shortly after Pete passed away, I had a phone message on our home answering machine that was rather long but filled with static. I listened to it over and over again, because I had a heightened sensation that it was Pete. When I sense something unusual, the hair on my arms stands up and I get goose bumps. If anyone could pull that off from heaven, it would be Pete. Because of the unusual loving events that had happened up to this point, I was beginning to wonder if God allowed our departed loved ones to comfort us and watch over us. Even though I could not make out any clear words, each time I listened to the static message, I had the strangest good feeling that it was Pete. The static message gave me the most wonderful goose bumps.

Wedding Bands
July 2013

In 2011 I lost the first wedding band that Pete bought me when we were married in 1989. I don't have knuckles and rings tend to slip off easily, and I don't like anything tight on me. I was overly conscientious about my wedding band being on, so I was surprised and upset when I realized it was missing. It was never found, but Pete replaced it with a second wedding band.

In late 2012, with Pete's diagnosis and the process he went through, I lost weight and my second wedding band was getting looser. I tend to talk with my hands a lot and at times when I was talking, my wedding band would go flying off. Pete asked me to get this second wedding band resized so that I wouldn't lose it too. I planned on getting it resized, but with all we were going through, it just didn't seem important. I was too focused on keeping him well.

After Pete was gone, I was also wearing his wedding band. It was several sizes larger than my largest finger. I had a rubber band wrapped around it to keep it on the middle finger of my right hand.

After his Celebration of Life service, I started the process of analyzing everything in his office. There were family items that I needed to find and get ready to distribute to family.

There was a chest of drawers in his closet that was in front of some items I needed. I looked to see what was in the chest and found that most of the drawers were empty with the exception of a couple of drawers, which had cards in it that were from me to Pete. I decided that I would put his cards in an armoire that was in his office and then I could get rid of the small chest of drawers.

Pete and I went crazy with cards for special occasions and didn't do just one card but usually four or five cards for each other. We would scatter them around the house for the occasions. After taking his cards from the small chest, I organized all our cards in the armoire. It was perfect and allowed me to remove the small chest of drawers from his closet.

On the shelves in his office closet were about 30 afghans and quilts that his mom had made. These were to be distributed to family. They were different sizes and precariously stacked on the shelves in the closet. I decided to organize them better until I could get them distributed to family. I thought if they were rolled and tied, they would be easier to stack by size. Pete had a six-foot folding table in his office that he used for putting jigsaw puzzles together. I used that table to roll and tie all the afghans and quilts and then stacked them back on the shelves in a more organized fashion.

I don't remember when I realized that I was missing his wedding band, but I assumed it had to be rolled up in one of the afghans or quilts. So, after spending quite a bit of time rolling, tying and stacking the afghans and quilts, I had to untie and unroll each one. I shook each one hoping the ring would appear. No ring. I believed it had to be in that room, but it could have been anywhere as I tend to multi-task. I was working on a variety of projects throughout the house.

In exasperation, I stood in his office and sort of stomped my foot and said, "Please help me find your ring. I just can't lose it." His ring gave me comfort, and I really did not want to lose it.

I suddenly felt directed to go to the armoire with the cards. I really didn't think it could be there as I thought I remembered having the ring when I was working on the cards, but I started removing the cards batch by batch laying them on the six-foot table in the room. As I was lifting a batch of cards from the armoire drawer, I heard a ping and saw his wedding ring rolling around on the floor.

I said a heart felt "thank you" for the direction and the finding. I also promised I would get his wedding band resized. I tied another rubber band around his wedding band so that I would not lose it again. I then had the task of re-organizing all the cards for a second time. I also had to roll, tie and stack the afghans and quilts for a second time.

Before I found a place to get his wedding band resized, I lost my own wedding band. I couldn't believe that I lost it, as I had just lost his wedding band even though I found his. I looked everywhere in the house, in the garage, in my car, in my work bag and my purse, but I could not find my wedding band. I figured it was like my first wedding band; it was just gone.

I found a jeweler that was recommended and took Pete's wedding band in to be resized. I told the jeweler that I had just lost my own wedding band and if I could find it, I would have it resized too.

It was about a week later and I had not picked up Pete's wedding band from the jeweler yet. I was preparing lunch at home. I had not eaten at home for the past week, as it was still too hard to eat at home alone. I opened a bag of spinach that I had eaten from the week before. It looked and smelled okay, so I grabbed a handful and dropped it onto my plate. I heard a "ping" as the spinach hit the plate. There, in the spinach, was my wedding band. I could almost feel Pete's presence on the other side of the kitchen counter and hear him laughing, and hear his words about getting the wedding band resized. I said I would get it resized.

When I took my wedding band into the jeweler, I shared with them where I found it. It gave them a good laugh. It was a first for them to hear someone lose a wedding band in spinach.

Heaven does have a sense of humor.

Security System
Summer 2013

At the last home that my husband and I shared we had a security system because of my business. It was a limited security system with motion detectors only. Pete really didn't want a complete system, as he didn't feel it was warranted in the community where we lived.

After he passed away, I was having a hard time sleeping. I did not feel secure. I knew I needed to do something to have peace of mind and feel secure enough to sleep.

Arrangements were made to upgrade the security system by adding the wireless sensors to all windows and doors. The first evening the system was upgraded, I set the alarm for the evening. Sometime around 8-8:30 pm the alarm went off. I went over to check the alarm and there was an error code. I disabled the alarming and it stopped. I didn't understand the error code at the time and the alarming had stopped, so I ignored it.

Fifteen minutes later the system alarm went off again. Once again I disabled the alarming and saw the same error message. I checked the alarm system manual for the error code but could not find it in the manual. I called the monitoring company, as I really didn't want the system alarming every fifteen minutes all night long.

The monitoring company told me the problem was not with my system but with the cell tower providing the service. They gave me a code to disable the whole system for the night so I could sleep. I could not believe that I had just upgraded the system that day so that I could have peace of mind and sleep, and now the whole system was shut down. It was a long night. The next morning I learned that it was resolved, and I was able to put the system back in operation.

A week later, I was sitting in my home office and one of the sensors on the shutters was loose and about ready to fall off. I took a picture of it and emailed it to the monitoring company. I asked what I needed to do to fix it. They did not want me to fix it; they arranged for one of their technicians to come out to fix it.

When the technician arrived, he fixed the sensor and checked out the entire system. I asked him about the alarming event that happened the day I had upgraded the system and the cell tower failure. He told me that in all the years he had been working with the company, it was only the second time that particular cell tower had failed. I asked him what cell tower. He told me it was the AT&T cell tower downtown that had failed.

I had to laugh because I instantly felt a connection to the alarm event and Pete. He was probably shaking his head at me for not having faith that I was secure and upgrading the system at a bit of an expense: During Pete's work with AT&T, one of his responsibilities was that cell tower. Coincidence? I don't think so. Hanging in my husband's office was a photo taken of that cell tower during a thunderstorm. His team had to climb to the top of that cell tower to repair something during the storm. Someone on his team took the photo.

I don't think Pete would have been upset by my decision to upgrade the security system. He told me to do whatever I needed to do to move forward in life. I think he was letting me know that he knew, and he was with me. It did give me a smile.

Church Surprises
October 27, 2013 and November 3, 2013

Sunday, October 27, 2013, would have been our 24th wedding anniversary. It was my first anniversary without Pete and all our crazy card sharing. Outside the sadness that he was not with me that day, all was well. I had started attending church at the Methodist Church where Pete worked as Security and Maintenance the last nine years of his life. They had been so supportive and wonderful to both of us during his illness. They had also given us the gift of a niche in the columbarium and provided his memorial service even though we were not members of the church.

During the church service that day, I had the sensation that someone on my left had just reached around me and a hand had squeezed my right shoulder. I was so startled that I looked to my right shoulder and then to my left to see who had just hugged me. Of course there was no one there. The hand felt like Pete's big gnarled hand. He had some sort of tendon issue with his hands and they would not open all the way so his hug around my shoulder was unique. Somehow, I knew he was there with me. It was a lovely "hug" from heaven for our 24th wedding anniversary.

The Sunday after our anniversary, November 3, 2013, was All Saints Sunday at the Methodist Church. The Methodist's have an annual tradition where they honor their church members who have passed away during the year.

The church notified me that they would be including my husband, Pete, in the All Saints Sunday service even though we were not members of the church. They considered Pete family because of his long employment with the church. I did not know what to expect. I was raised a Baptist and had only been attending the Methodist church for a couple of months, so I was still adjusting to the Methodist service format and practices.

On that Sunday I was at church and sitting in the back, which was my habit at that time. Just before the service started, I heard someone call my name, "Lynn." I turned around and there was my brother. I was surprised as he was an active member at another local church. He said, "I decided to surprise you and join you for church today." He knew nothing about this service, as I had not shared it with him or anyone else.

The All Saints Sunday service started with members of the church carrying in a single candle in a little glass candleholder, which represented each member that had passed away during the year. All the candles were placed at the front of the church in a beautiful array. The pastors then called out all the names of those who had passed away and shared scripture from Revelations about saints. It was a lovely ceremony.

Then the senior pastor started preaching on "Celebrating Life" and shared about Pete and his positive outlook on life. Stunned and visibly shaken by the beautiful message she shared about my husband's life attitude, I could not contain my tears and emotions.

After the service, my brother and I went to lunch. I knew the church did not know him, so I asked him what prompted him to be with me on this particular Sunday. He said, "Yesterday God said I should surprise you and attend church with you." Coincidence? I believe in my heart that God sent my brother, as he knew I would need to be comforted.

Also unknown to anyone, including my brother, November 3rd was Pete's mom's birthday. Pete's mom, Anna, passed away a few hours after her 102 or 103 birthday in 2003. We were never sure about the year of her birth, as there were conflicting documents.

With the anniversary hug at church on our wedding anniversary and then the beautiful tribute to Pete the following Sunday, which was also his mom's birthday, I had the most loving sense of Pete and Anna's presence and the presence of a loving heavenly father.

The First Visit
December 15, 2013

One of Pete's jobs at the Methodist Church had been to open and close the church each day. On Sunday mornings, he would open the church and get it ready for the morning services. He would then come home and put his keys and billfold on the kitchen bar counter and put his coat on a chair. In the winter, I could always feel the cold air that he would bring in with him and smell the essence of Pete in the cold air. Everyone has their scent, and Pete had a lovely scent between his aftershave and his sweet sweat.

After he got home, we would watch a church service together online. We didn't try to attend a church because invariably Pete would get a call from the Methodist church that something wasn't working, and he would have to return to the church to take care of the problem.

On Sunday, December 15, 2013, I was running a little behind on getting ready to go to church. As I came from the bedroom through the great room towards my office to gather my purse and bible, I felt the cold air and smelled the essence of Pete. It was just like when he came home after opening the church on cold Sunday mornings. It was at the exact spot where he would put his keys and billfold on the counter. It seemed so real, I remember saying, "Oh, Sweetie Petey" as I moved quickly around the area to my office. I kept moving and left the house.

About a block from home, I realized what had just happened. I had smelled him and sensed his presence, and I had actually talked to him as if he were there. At that moment, I cried.

It was such an emotional encounter, that I had a hard time keeping it all together at church and for the rest of the day. That evening I went to a Christmas concert with my neighbor and some of her friends. I got separated from them, which was a blessing because I cried through the whole concert.

I know in my heart that his visit was to show me love and that he was with me. This was my first holiday season without Pete.

2014

Change and Loving Help

The Walker Incident
January 25, 2014

About a week or so after my husband passed away in 2013, I noticed a new walker that came by our home. My desk was arranged in my office so that I could look outside. I enjoyed watching people come and go as I worked. This new walker had to be someone new in the community as I was pretty tuned in to the people traffic that went up and down our street.

Everyday like clock work this guy would come by. Something about this walker intrigued me. I finally realized that I felt the essence of Pete in this guy. His walking mannerism, his arms and his whole attitude resembled Pete's.

I started calling this guy "my smile guy." He never smiled but he made me smile. Why? I have no idea except I felt Pete's presence when this guy walked by. This was especially true when one day he walked by and he had on a head sweatband and a tank top just like Pete used to wear. Over the months I looked forward to seeing this guy just because I sensed Pete's presence when he came by the house.

On Saturday, January 25, 2014, this guy walked by the house as usual, and I am not sure why but the feeling of Pete was so strong that I jumped up out of my office chair with this strange excitement and said out loud, "My smile guy!" At that moment I heard a "pop."

A little later I realized that the house was cold. It was a cold January morning and I had the furnace running. I went to the thermostat and it was blank. I tried to turn it on but nothing was happening. I got out the thermostat manual for suggestions on troubleshooting. I replaced the batteries to the thermostat, checked the circuit breaker, and power switch to the heating/cooling system, but the thermostat was still blank.

I called the man we used for doing the semi-annual checks on our heating and cooling system. When I reached him, he and his family were on a weekend outing. He could not get to me until Monday morning.

When he came on Monday morning, he told me that the thermostat had to be replaced. That "pop" I heard just after I said the words "my smile guy" with so much excitement was the thermostat. Coincidence? I don't think so.

I was a little more careful after that about what I said when "my smile guy" walked by. He continued to walk by almost daily until the day I no longer owned this last home that Pete and I had shared together.

Looking back, I believe this guy's walking by each day since Pete's passing, and the feeling of Pete's presence when he did walk by, was another sign from heaven to show me that I was being watched over every day.

Emotions
February 5, 2014

About a week before Valentine's Day and I found myself a really blue. Not that Valentine's Day was a special day for Pete and I. We celebrated Valentine's Day everyday by loving and caring for each other. We weren't a perfect couple, but almost perfect! We had a beautiful marriage.

I had noticed since Christmas that I was starting to have some depression. The reality of Pete not physically coming back was hitting me hard. I found myself cancelling appointments because of my emotions. On this February day I cancelled all my appointments. I knew I could not face my customers that day.

It was a cold and grey day, which didn't help my emotional state. I was sitting in my office, which faces the street, when I saw a nice black car pull up in front of our driveway blocking the entire driveway. I thought that rather odd. A guy got out and he had on a short sleeve shirt and no coat. He was carrying a small bag. He totally ignored the "No Solicitation" sign at the gate and came through the gate towards the front door.

Now, I was curious as to why a stranger would block the driveway, was wearing a short sleeve shirt when it was cold outside and completely ignored the "No Solicitation" sign. I went to the front door and opened the inner door. The outer security screen door was locked.

The man introduced himself as an Area Ambassador for a large church in Georgia that Pete and I had supported. We watched the church services online on Sundays. This man indicated that they wanted to "Thank" us for partnering with them, and they had a gift for us. He must have sensed that I was not in the best of spirits and uncomfortable in opening the outer door, as he offered to put the gift bag on the handle of the outer door.

I don't know why, but I opened the door, stepped outside and took the bag. I "thanked" him for the gift and for stopping by. I think I "thanked" him two or three times, but I couldn't say anything else because I knew I would cry.

After he left, I returned to my office and I opened the gift bag. There was a book written by the Pastor of the church entitled "Emotions." The Area Ambassador's business card was in the book directly on a chapter about the "emotions of grief or despair." At that moment, I knew God had just given me a "God hug." I cried.

Later that day I wrote the Area Ambassador an email "thanking" him again. I explained the timing of his visit and what I had been experiencing. This church was not aware that Pete had passed away as I had not shared this with them. We were not members of the church. We just watched the service online each Sunday and supported them.

This man and this gift were sent to help me. I don't remember everything I read in the book, but it gave me the insight to realize that my current home caused much of my depression. It was the last home Pete and I shared together. It was one of the happiest times of our lives. We were both active helping people in various ways and our marriage was a joy. But now that Pete was gone, I was having more difficulty finding happiness in the house.

The timing of this man's visit and his gift was exactly what I needed at the moment. God was showing me that it was time to start a new journey.

Dog Behavior
February 14, 2014

I have always sensed that animals see things that we can't see. My own dog, that I had for 15 years, showed me a little of this, but at the time I didn't fully understand.

One of my customers had a cute little dog that came into her life by accident. This little dog was found running around her senior neighborhood. The neighbors were out trying to catch the little dog to see if they could find its home before coyotes discovered it. My customer took the little dog in while postings were made throughout the community regarding the dog. No one claimed the dog and it had no tags or embedded chip. My customer fell in love with the little dog and adopted it as her own.

When I came to her home, her dog would bark at me when I first arrived and then would disappear. I would not see this dog for the rest of my visit with my customer. This pattern had been going on for several years.

On Valentine's Day in February 2014, the dog did its normal barking at me when I arrived, but what it did next baffled both the owner and myself. The owner and I had settled in the kitchen to work on her technology devices.

I had just sat down and her little dog jumped up into my lap. The owner and I were both surprised, and the owner told the dog to get down. The dog did not want to get down. I told the owner it was okay. I could work with her dog in my lap. It was a cute little cuddly dog, and I was happy to have it in my lap.

Her dog curled up in my lap, but every few minutes she looked up at me and then looked up above my head. She cocked her head and looked to each side of the area above my head. She then settled back down on my lap. This pattern continued. My customer also noticed the behavior.

I assumed my customer knew I had lost Pete. I told her I felt like someone was with us, and her dog was seeing this presence. I wasn't sure how my customer would handle that statement, so I continued to share with her that I had sensed Pete's presence around me at times since his passing.

My customer was shocked. She was not aware that Pete had passed away. He had helped her for my business, and he had done handyman work for her while working for another local service organization.

She said she noticed her dog was seeing something but thought it might be her deceased husband. She sensed her husband's presence in this home at times. It was her husband's favorite home. This was Valentine's Day so it might possibly have been my husband, Pete, and/or my customer's husband there with us. It gave us smiles.

I had a similar experience with my sister's dog at another time after that experience. My sister had her dachshund on her lap, and I was sitting across from her and her dog. My parents, brother and sister-in-law were also sitting around the room. My sister's dog suddenly looked up above my head and did the same kind of looking to each side above my head. I did not say anything at the time because I was not sure how my family would handle it. They did not seem to notice the dog's behavior.

I had a nice warm feeling on both of those occasions. I sensed there was some heavenly presence there watching over us.

Should I Stay or Should I Go?
March 2014

After the visit from the Area Ambassador of the Georgia church and the gift of the book, "Emotions," I knew I needed to move from the last home Pete and I shared.

I started looking casually online at different properties. There is a saying that "sometimes the grass is not greener on the other side." In looking at other properties, I hoped I might realize that the best home for me was my current home. That wasn't the case. I was feeling the need to move even more.

One day I just sat quietly and wrote on a piece of paper the words, "Should I stay or should I go?" Immediately I heard the words, "In time, I will guide you." I wrote those words down. I didn't know what they meant at the time. I just wrote what I heard.

Shortly after that I kept getting this nudging that I needed to get rid of stuff. It was almost like a command. I remembered that Pete had said to me near the end of his life that I should keep what I needed, wanted, what was sentimental, and let everything else go. Looking back, I believe it was his way of helping me work through all his tools and other stuff.

Stephanie Lynn Funk

I thought I had already gone through quite a bit of downsizing and simplifying after Pete was gone, but there was this constant nudge to look again. So again I would go through every drawer, every cabinet, my clothes, and I assessed every piece of furniture. Anything that I had not used or wore in a while, I put out in the garage. I made a commitment to myself that if I put something out in the garage, I would not take back in the house; so I made sure I didn't want items before putting them in the garage. I was so surprised at the amount of stuff that we had accumulated that really had no meaningful value now, and I had already gotten rid of a lot of stuff or so I thought.

In the meantime, I continued looking at properties online. One piece of property kept popping up in my queries. I kept saying, "But God it is long and skinny," and I kept getting the strange words, "You need to step inside." It had the options that I wanted in a property; it just looked long and skinny from the online photos.

I asked my step-daughter, who is a broker, if she would find out what realtor actually held the property and see if I could just step inside. I shared with her what I thought about the property, and this strange command that I kept getting. She contacted the realtor and arrangements were made for me to look at the property.

On Friday, April 4, 2014, I went to the property. I arrived before the realtor. While standing outside, there was a lovely little breeze. A large Sissoo tree in the front yard was enjoying the breeze. I still had this "long and skinny" in my head, but there was something very welcoming while I waited for the realtor. When the realtor arrived, we went inside. The moment I stepped inside, I said to myself, "It isn't long and skinny." The realtor would not have understood that comment. At that moment I knew that villa was mine.

But God wasn't done with me yet on this villa. The next couple of months would test my faith. But, I knew it was time for me to sell my home and prepare to move. I was fulfilling the nudging to get rid of stuff and simplify my life. I was beginning to understand the meaning of the words, "In time, I will guide you."

The Villa, My Faith, The Gift
June 4, 2014

On April 11, 2014, I put the last home Pete and I shared together on the market. I had found a villa in another community the week before that I felt God had led me to, and I believed that it was mine.

I assumed that if God wanted me to have the villa, He was going to sell my home quickly so that I could buy the villa. Well, that wasn't quite what He had in mind. My faith was going to be tested. The owner of the villa did not want to work with me, as she had a previous disappointment with selling the villa and did not want to be disappointed again. For me to buy the villa, I had to sell my home.

I communicated weekly with the Realtor selling the villa. She knew I wanted that villa. Two times between April 4, 2014, and June 3, 2014, the villa almost sold. The realtor kept my stepdaughter, who is a broker, abreast of each of these occurrences. The second time the villa almost sold, I cried out to God. I didn't understand. However, both times the sale of the villa fell through; the buyers walked away. It was as if God was telling me to have faith; He was in control.

On June 3, 2014, my stepdaughter wrote me an email that the villa had yet another offer, and it looked like this one would probably go through. She said the realtor had another villa model I might be interested in that would be on the market soon. I was devastated, and I was angry. I was not interested in the other villa model, and I was so sure that the particular villa God showed me was supposed to be mine! At this point, I really did not understand. My emotions were a mixed bag of hurt, disappointment, and anger. I could not handle the yo-yo effect on my emotions, so I asked God to take away the villa. I wasn't sure what I was going to do, but I could not handle the up and down of my emotions.

At the moment that I asked God to take away the villa, I felt as if I was told to call my brother. My brother had been such a help to me since Pete's passing. He had offered to loan me the money earlier so that I could buy the villa, but I had turned him down. I had always felt if God wanted me to have the villa, He would sell my home. Now, it seemed that God wanted me to learn to let others help me. I called my brother but he was not home, so I left a message.

On the morning of June 4, 2014, my brother called me and told me he would loan me the money. I called my stepdaughter and asked her to make an offer on the villa to see if we could override the other offer.

I took the day off from my business, as I knew it was going to be a difficult day. My emotions were on a roller coaster from all the ups and downs on the sale of my house and the villa that I thought God wanted me to have. My house had been on the market for two months. I had a lot of viewings on the house but had not landed an offer. About 10 in the morning I got a call from a realtor asking if she could show my house at 11 am. Realtors called me to make sure the security system was off. I left the house around 10:30 am.

I was having lunch when I got a call from my stepdaughter, who was brokering both the villa that I wanted and my home that was for sale. She shared with me that my offer on the villa had been accepted. She then told me that I had an offer on my house. I had to pause to take it all in, that I had both the villa and an offer on my house.

This was not an ordinary circumstance. June 4, 2014, was the first anniversary of Pete's passing. He always wanted to celebrate life, and he would have only wanted a celebration on the anniversary of his passing. This gift of the villa and the sale of our last home together on the anniversary of his passing would have been exactly what he would have wanted for me. What a beautiful "hug" from heaven and one that I will never forget.

From that day June 4 through June 7, 2014, it was as if my house was a "hotcake" on the real estate market. The volume of calls to see the house was more than in the previous two months. It got to be kind of funny. Even my stepdaughter chuckled at what was happening. This was also a humbling experience in that I had allowed my faith to waiver and had not trusted that God was in total control.

The Reading
May 10, 2014

For most of my adult life, I was led to believe that mediums should not to be taken seriously. In late 2013 a friend learned of Pete's passing and sent me a book she thought might help me in my grief. Her son had committed suicide, and she found comfort through that book. When I saw that the book was written by a medium, I wasn't sure about reading it. I prayed about it and asked God to help me only know the truth. I was floored when I read the book, as I realized that I had many of the same spiritual experiences as the author. I was still having those spiritual experiences. God was showing me something about myself. I was reminded about being told three times in my life that I had a gift of knowing and the ability to receive and understand information. I ignored or blocked it because I could not handle it. I only used the information at times when I felt threatened or it was useful for the moment. It did help in those situations. I never shared this with anyone except Pete, and only because of some events that occurred that helped us at the time.

In May 2014 one of my stepdaughters was having difficulty processing Pete's passing and knowing that he was okay. Her husband bought her tickets to see a well-known local medium. It was a fairly large event of about 200 people. The medium told the group that she would be able to do about 10 or 11 readings in the time she had with them. She selected my stepdaughter for a reading. At that moment, my stepdaughter's husband started recording the interaction between the medium and my stepdaughter.

The medium asked my stepdaughter whom she was trying to connect with and she said, "My dad." The medium must have sensed there was more than one dad, and she asked that question. My stepdaughter responded that this was her stepdad, but she emphatically stated he was her real dad. The medium asked if this was the only dad that had passed, and my stepdaughter responded, "Yes." There was a slight pause, and then the medium started laughing and commented that he was quite humorous. She told my stepdaughter that when her dad (my husband Pete) went to heaven he reverted back to 33. She asked my stepdaughter if this made sense to her; it did not make sense to her.

After the event, my stepdaughter and her husband called me to share what they had learned, and to give me a message that was directed at me. When they shared about Pete reverting back to 33, I cried. I knew exactly what it meant. Immediately, I was reminded of a casual discussion Pete and I had in 2010 or 2011. Pete and I had finished reading a book about a young boy that had a heaven experience. On one of our many casual discussions, we were talking about the boy in the book seeing his great grandfather in heaven, not at the older age when his great grandfather had passed away, but as a younger man. This boy never knew his great grandfather because his great grandfather passed way almost a quarter of a century before the boy was born. During our discussion, Pete told me that if one of the rewards in heaven was to roll back to an earlier age, he wanted to roll back to 33 when he went to heaven. I was surprised by 33 and asked him, "Why 33"? He said, "I want to be the age of Jesus when He went to the cross." I had forgotten about that discussion until this medium revelation. It was as if heaven wanted me to know that Pete got his desire to roll back to 33.

My whole way of thinking about heaven was shifting. I was starting to understand that there is more interaction between heaven and those of us still engaged in this physical life in ways I could not even fathom before. We only needed to be open and receptive to the love and help.

I was also starting to see a shift in my understanding of mediums.

Sewing Help
Spring 2014

Sewing was never my strength. In Junior High School we had to take sewing for Home Economics. I got a D in sewing. I had ripped out a zipper in a skirt so many times that by the time the zipper was correct, the skirt had holes from all the times I had to rip out the zipper. I have attempted to sew off and on over the years, but the art of sewing has eluded me. I do mend or sew buttons back on but that's about it.

Sometime in the spring of 2014 I had a shirt that needed a button sewed back on it. The shirt was an odd color of burgundy or maroon, and if the thread was not the right color, it was going to show. In my sewing kit, I had lots of these little tiny spools of thread in all different colors and shades of colors, but none of the burgundy or maroon shades were a match.

Something told me to check Anna's plastic container of sewing items. Anna was my wonderful mother-in-law. When we needed to dismantle her home, she had a plastic storage box with some of her sewing items. I kept this plastic storage box and an old carry-on airline bag filled with buttons. This plastic container and the bag of buttons were in the closet next to my sewing box.

I got out Anna's plastic sewing container and opened it. I could not believe what I was seeing. Right there in front of me on top was the perfect color of thread! After starring briefly at this in disbelief, I said, "Thank you, Anna" and sewed my button back on. It was perfect. I felt her presence there that day, as if she was helping me to sew. The button was perfectly positioned on the shirt and looked fantastic.

Hummingbirds To My Left
Spring 2014

Outside of our fascination with roadrunners, Pete and I were not really drawn to birds in any special way. When we were running, we talked about everything, but rarely about birds unless it was the sighting of a roadrunner. I had not been out running since before Pete passed away. It was difficult for me to push myself to go back outside running after running with Pete for almost 25 years.

Around March of 2014 I finally stepped outside to run. I had been running about a week when I noticed that about a half mile down the street a hummingbird swooped out in front of me from my left and did this little song and dance in front of me. It flew up high and then came back down low and fluttered a little longer in front of me. It did this a couple of times before leaving me. I was startled by the hummingbird, but didn't give it much thought until it continued to happen almost on a daily basis. I had this strange sensation that this was not an ordinary occurrence.

I started going down the same path everyday, and sure enough on the post of a street sign about a half-mile from home would be this hummingbird. As soon as I approached, it would fly out in front of me and do its little song and dance. Up in the air and then down, and side-to-side, and then up again and down again, and then hovering. It was like a little dance. Some days the hummingbird was more energetic than other days, but it was almost always there. I found myself greeting and talking to this hummingbird and blowing it kisses as it left me each day. I had never had an experience with hummingbirds like this before. I had this intuitive sense of some presence with me. I felt such happiness with the presence of my almost daily hummingbird ritual.

This went on from March 2014 through June 28, 2014. This was the day I moved from the house Pete and I shared to a new home in another community about eight miles away. I needed to move my life forward, but I knew I was going to miss the entertainment and joy of my hummingbird ritual.

It took me a little over a week to unpack and get settled in my new community and to look at the street layout before I took my first run. I had been running in the community about a week when in the first mile from my left came this hummingbird, and it did the same song and dance. To say I was stunned would be an understatement! Up and down it went, then side-to-side, and then a second time, and a hovering before leaving me. I could not believe what I was seeing, but I was overjoyed. Everyday around my first mile, at the same place, this hummingbird would appear from my left and entertain me. I would greet it, talk to it and blow it kisses when it was time for it to go. I always had this wonderful sense of a loving presence.

On July 24, 2014, I went out for my run. I had a lot on my mind because it was closing day on the last home I shared with Pete. I had run past mile one and was clearly into my second mile when I realized I had missed my hummingbird.

I no sooner made that mental thought than from my left a hummingbird appeared and did the usual song and dance. Up and down in front of me it went and then again, then it hovered and flew away. This time though the hummingbird flew to a tree about a half block in front of me on my left. As I approached the tree, it came back out again and flew up and down, side to side, and then hovered which I knew was a sign that it would be leaving me.

On this day as the hummingbird came the second time, I heard these mental words, "Even if you don't see me everyday, it doesn't mean I am not with you." I had to reflect on that message. It seemed that the message wanted me to see that I didn't need a physical crutch to know that I was loved from heaven.

I have had many more hummingbird experiences. It seems to be the ones that approach from the left and their presence always gives me the most awesome feeling of love and goose bumps.

Hummingbirds
& Customers
October/November 2014

Hummingbirds had become an important part of my life. I never dreamed that they would mean so much to me. I have read and heard about hummingbirds bringing comfort and joy, but I had never experienced that before until the spring of 2014. Maybe it was their energy. They seem to vibrate at a high level of energy.

On October 15, 2014, I was sitting in my favorite space in my office where I can look out the window and see a segment of the heavens. The sky was beautiful that morning with light fluffy clouds. On this particular morning, I thanked God for all the hummingbirds that He had shared with me. I had felt so much joy in the presence of hummingbirds.

In my little segment of sky that I could see from my sitting area, just after I had thanked God for all the hummingbirds, there appeared a cloud formation that was a hummingbird. I was awe struck! I had just thanked Him for hummingbirds and here was a beautiful cloud formation of a hummingbird. I was still joyous over the first cloud formation when another cloud formation of another hummingbird appeared! Two cloud formations in one morning! What a lovely big "hug" from heaven.

On October 28, 2014, I was at one of my long-term customer's home. Her office has a large window in front of her work area. We were working away and she was talking to me, but I was fascinated by what I was seeing outside the window. There was a hummingbird that kept flitting in front of the window and then a butterfly joined it, and the two are doing a little song and dance in front of the window together. I felt a very strange connection. It was as if they were trying to convey a message to me, but I wasn't getting it. I was having a difficult time concentrating on what my customer was trying to tell me. The behavior of the hummingbird and butterfly was clearly not normal. I later shared with my customer what had been fascinating me. She said she knew I was distracted but didn't realize what was distracting me.

The following week, the first week in November, I was at another long-term customer home and her office also has a large window in front of her work area. It was close to sundown and all of a sudden a hummingbird began buzzing the window and flitting frantically at the window. It then swooped up to the roof of the house next door and then came back to our window and did this song and dance. It was the same song and dance of the hummingbirds that impact me the most. I had this strange sensation that this hummingbird's unusual behavior was trying to convey something to me. My customer also noticed the unusual activity of the hummingbird. I shared with this customer how I had been having a lot of hummingbird activity and almost always when they came from my left. This one and the one the week before presented from the left.

During this time period, I was struggling with a landscape issue and having difficulty in knowing what to do. It all unraveled in the next several weeks with more divine intervention of rainbows and birds.

Landscape, Owl, Hummingbird and Rainbow
December 2014

The second year after losing Pete seemed to be harder than the first year, especially around the holidays. It was the first week in December 2014. I was out on my morning run and mentally talking to God about my landscape problem. I had two large messy trees and both were infringing on neighboring yards. I had already called my landscaper twice. I left a message both times, but he had not called me back. The two phone calls were over the course of a few weeks to a month. I was not used to handling vendors for the home. This was always done by my husband, Pete, and in my old neighborhood, a neighbor stepped in just before I sold the house to assist with the landscape. I found it difficult to ask for help and was not comfortable dealing with the trades.

I had learned about this landscaper shortly after moving into my villa a few months earlier. I had a leak and a neighbor saw my dilemma and recommended this local landscaper. The landscaper happened to be in the neighborhood and came over and fixed my leak. I felt comfortable that I had a landscaper, so when he wasn't answering my calls, I wasn't sure what to do.

That morning it was cloudy while I was running. As I was rounding my last mile towards home, the sun peeped out somewhere in the east and a beautiful rainbow appeared. The rainbow gave me faith to understand that God knew my needs and heard my heart. I also heard a message that said to call the landscaper again. Now I found myself arguing with God saying, "But I have already called him twice, and he hasn't answered." The message was "call him again." God can be persistent.

When I got home, I called the landscaper again and left a message. I have no idea why I said what I said, but I think someone else was guiding my tongue. I said, "Tom, did you forget me?" Then I left my name and number. I hung up and could not believe I had just said those words.

It was a couple of days after my third call to the landscaper, and I still had not heard from him. It was raining and after my morning devotions, I felt a prompting that I was to go to the garage. I didn't know why I was going to the garage but I went. I have learned when I get these strange promptings, that it is best to follow them. I opened the garage door and the smell of the rain was heavenly. God just wanted me to take in the beauty of the rain. I leaned against the back of my car and just enjoyed the rain and the morning.

A couple of minutes into enjoying the rain, a truck pulled up, the window on the passenger side went down and it was my landscaper who said, "I haven't forgotten you. I will take care of your yard next week." The window of the truck went up and he drove off. I thanked God and cried.

The next day I was at a customer home. We were sitting in their office, which had a lovely window to their back yard. There was a little sparrow playing in the bush just outside the window. It sat on a limb and looked into the window for the longest time and kept cocking its head as if it was listening to our conversation. We laughed about this bird and its strange behavior, but I had the strange intuitive sense that this was another heavenly presence. The sparrow was also on my left. It was quite entertaining and gave us all smiles.

The following day I was sitting at my desk in my office, which faces the window. Most of my view from my desk is the villa next door. Our homes are quite close and there isn't any vegetation between the houses, so I don't see many birds from my office window. This particular morning two birds, I did not recognize, appeared on the tile roofline just across from my window. They almost looked like female cardinals, but we don't see many cardinals in this part of the valley. All of a sudden, one of the birds flew right up to my window. I was worried it was going to hit the window. It fluttered at the window and then flew back up to the roofline of the villa next-door and just sat there looking in the window. Again, I had the strangest intuitive sensation about these two birds. It was almost as if they were trying to give me a message.

The following day I had just finished my devotions, and the doorbell rang. It was the landscaper. He asked if I had a camera. There was a huge owl sitting in the overgrown Sissoo tree in my front yard. This tree was so huge and the foliage so dense that I did not realize that the owl had been visiting my tree for sometime. My landscaper showed me the evidence on the ground of its long-term presence in the tree. This owl was one of the largest I have seen.

At first it appeared to be sleeping, but as more neighbors came to look at it, it opened its eyes. As I was taking pictures of it, it turned its head and looked right into the camera. A few minutes later a hummingbird approached the owl from the left. It buzzed frantically around the owl. I was not able to capture that moment as I had just lowered my camera before the hummingbird appeared. I was so surprised as were the neighbors. We could not believe that a hummingbird would aggravate a huge owl. The owl just ignored it, and the hummingbird flew off before I could get my camera up to get a picture.

When the landscaper started cutting into the branches of the tree, the owl decided it was time to leave. It was so large that it almost touched the ground trying to get enough momentum to get in the air.

The following day's Daily Word devotional reading had an "owl" in the picture for the reading. I felt a deep sense of joy and gratitude as I reflected on the week's events with all the birds and knew that God hadn't forgotten me, and my landscape needs had been taken care of with entertainment and joy.

2015

More Decisions with Help and Humor

Snoopy
January through September 2015

After the holidays I was feeling restless again. My business was consuming me, and I had no life. I had a technology service business and all my customers were seniors, meaning they were mostly over seventy. I taught all types of technology and was a troubleshooter for all types of technology. I also took care of several senior community businesses that included website building and maintenance as well as caring for their networks. My days were spent either at a customer home or business or I was home doing email or phone work with my customers. It had become a 24/7 operation. I felt there had to be more to life than technology.

What I am sharing on this event is hard to explain, because I have no idea how this could happen and I still don't, but I am constantly reminded that with God anything is possible. So, I leave it at that and I am sharing from my heart what transpired.

In January 2015 I noticed that one of the Snoopy figurines that was sitting on my file cabinet had moved. The Snoopy figurines were from my husband's collection. He loved Snoopy and had quite a collection of Snoopy memorabilia. On his desk he had three small Snoopy figurines that I kept and put in my office. I had them on top of a heavy 4-draw file cabinet that was next to my desk. They were lined up with a little resin Snoopy on the left with a larger ceramic bobble-head Snoopy in the middle and then a smaller pewter Snoopy on the right.

The resin Snoopy had a flower in its hand that a little girl gave me at my husband, Pete's, Celebration of Life service. I didn't know what to do with the little flower until I saw the hole in the resin Snoopy's hand so I stuck it in Snoopy's hand back in 2013.

These three Snoopy figurines had been sitting on my file cabinet since I moved to the villa in June 2014. There had not been anything unusual with them until January 2015.

On January 22, 2015, the resin Snoopy was not in line with the other Snoopy figurines and was turned so that the flower was pointing towards my desk in line with where I sat. It was almost as if Snoopy was presenting me with the flower. I thought how cute, and I don't know what possessed me but I took a picture of it. I didn't think much of this and after I took the photo, I put the resin Snoopy back in line with the others.

Periodically, I would find that the resin Snoopy had moved a little. I would just let it go, and I kept taking photos of what I was seeing. After the Snoopy was turned where the flower was presenting itself to me, the movement stopped.

I would then move it back to see if it would happen again. I was fascinated and as I am a curious person, I was trying to figure out what could be causing the movement of this one object on my filing cabinet when nothing else was moving.

At one point in trying to figure this out, I barricaded the foot of the resin Snoopy near the front side of the larger, heavier ceramic Snoopy to see if that would stop the movement; it did not! The resin Snoopy continued to move behind and rotate so that the flower presented toward my desk and then the movement would stop.

All this went on until the last time I recorded movement on September 6, 2015. There was no more movement after this. It just stopped. As I was writing this book, I realized that even though the movement had stopped, during the time all of this was happening, from January through September, it brought me joy and I felt a sense of love each time the Snoopy was turned towards my desk pointing that flower at me. I was going through another transition period and needed to make a difficult decision on whether to continue my business or let it go, and this moving Snoopy helped ease the stress. It diverted my thoughts from my business to something that gave me smiles. It would have been something my Pete would have done to give me a smile.

Later when I looked at the series of photos I had taken of all this movement, I realized that the first time I noticed this resin Snoopy presenting the flower and I took the first photo, it was my husband's birthday, January 22nd!

January 22, 2015 – First Snoopy Photo

Wind Hugs
June 2015

Have you ever felt a "wind hug?" I had not really even thought about the wind hugging me until several events happened where there was no wind, but there was a little breeze circling around me.

The first time I noticed this and made a note in my journal was on June 13, 2015. I was outside at the corner of my villa. I was stretching my legs after my morning run on a large rock. I felt a little breeze whirling around me but the leaves on the trees and shrubs around me were not moving. I had this lovely sensation that I was being hugged and I had a feeling of happiness. When I have these sensations, I usually have goose bumps or the hair on my arms stands up. I had goose bumps as if I was chilled, and it was warm outside.

That same week, mid-morning, I was sitting in my office with the window open and I heard my name being called. I went to the window to see if someone was calling my name from the front sidewalk, as my office window is close to the front of the house. There was no one there. I went to the front door and looked out and there was no one. I checked at the back patio door, as it was open too. There was no one but I heard my name loud and clear. I did not recognize the voice just my name.

June 28, 2015, after church I stopped in the columbarium where Pete's ashes are located. I was standing in front of his "niche" with my hands on the "niche" singing a silly little song that I always sang to him, when I felt that strange breeze wrapping around me. It was a still day; there was no wind just this loving breeze around me. I started calling these "my wind hugs."

Looking back, I don't really know what to think on hearing my name being called, but it was crystal clear. It was just like the voice that yelled at me back in 1993. Was it the wind calling my name? Another type of "wind hug?" Because this event happened in the same time period as the two "wind hugs," I sensed they were connected and maybe someday I will understand.

The "wind hugs" are not often, but when they happen, they are lovely and I get goose bumps.

Running Tease
Summer 2015

Pete used to tease me while we were running. There was one thing that he did that my reaction always got a chuckle out of him. He usually ran on my left and it would be when I was preoccupied in conversation or thought that he would yank my shorts. This would cause them to come down a bit. He almost always caught me off guard when he did this, which caused a reaction on my part, which tickled him.

What I am sharing are those "how could this happen" type of events, but then God reminds me that with Him anything is possible.

It was the summer of 2015, and I was running one of my longer routes, and I was in the "runner's zone." For those who are not runners, there is a phenomenon that happens after a runner gets going in running. After the breathing gets in sync, the mind goes floating off into space, deep in thought. It is a great time to solve problems or be creative.

I was in one of those "zones" when all of a sudden I felt a tug at my shorts on my left. It was a strong enough tug that it caused my shorts to slip just like they did when Pete would yank them. I whirled around to see who had just tugged my shorts, and no one was there but a yucca bush. I could only guess that a branch had somehow connected with my shorts.

I was surprised that it was strong enough to actually cause my shorts to come down a bit. I had this strange sensation that Pete was standing there laughing. I went on my way, but now my mind was more on the event that just happened then on whatever thought I was engaged with before the event.

Later in the summer I was again running on a longer route and was in my "zone." It happened again. My shorts were tugged on the left and they came down a bit. I whirled around and I was in the same area with the same yucca bush! I couldn't believe that it happened again, and I had this strange sensation that Pete was standing there laughing.

I was talking to myself, but I let that yucca bush know that I would be more careful when approaching it in the future since it seemed to have Pete's wicked sense of humor. After that when I was in that area, I was more tuned into the yucca bush as I approached it. I still had a feeling that Pete was there, and I would high five at the edge of the bush where I felt his presence.

I am glad that heaven has a sense of humor.

Tulip Chime
August 2015

Tulips have been my favorite flower since I was a child, and I have a lot of tulips of all types around the house and my office. When it came to gifts, Pete knew he couldn't go wrong with tulips.

Pete made me picket fences that had stapled tulip bushes coming from behind making it look like the tulips were growing through the picket fences. I had a tulip chime hanging from one of the picket fences. The tulip chime was designed to be outdoors, but it was so cute I kept it in the house in different places. It had been hanging on this picket fence since I moved to the villa in 2014. The bell on it was so heavy that it never dinged. It moved slightly on occasion, but there just wasn't enough breeze from any source to get it to ding.

On August 16, 2015, in my morning prayer and meditation time, the tulip chime actually dinged. I was sitting in a chair about two feet from where the chime hung. I looked at it and it was moving, but it only dinged once. On three mornings of that same week during my meditation and prayer time, the tulip chime dinged, but just one ding on each occasion.

When it happened, my mind went into logic mode trying to figure out all the reasons why it shouldn't have happened or

Stephanie Lynn Funk

what might have caused it to happen, but there just wasn't any logic. When I go into logic mode, I often hear the words "Don't put Me (meaning God) in a box" or the words "With Me (God) nothing is impossible." It seemed to be God's way of letting me know He heard my prayers, and I was to have faith and believe that with Him all things are possible.

On the morning of September 24, 2015, I was drying my hair, and I heard a clear voice say, "I am here." It was so strong and real that I looked around, and no one was there. I felt Pete's presence. It was not as if I heard his voice, it was the essence of him that I felt. I just started talking to him as if he was there. I was sharing with him how much I missed him, and how much I needed his help in making a decision regarding letting go of my business and moving forward in my life. While I was talking to him, I heard the little tulip chime in my office ding again—just one time.

The tulip chime did not ding again until two years later on October 15, 2017. It was again during my morning meditation and prayer time, and again only one ding. As of this writing, I have never heard it ding again.

Electricity and Warning
August 24, 2015

For 15 years I had a technology business that served seniors and senior businesses. My services included teaching the "how to" on all types of devices and software, as well as troubleshooting and providing support. I was often asked to do other related electronic tasks for customers, which I would gladly do if I had the skill and knowledge.

On August 24, 2015, I was at a customer home and had taken care of her technology needs. She asked me if I knew anything about 5-CD changers. I was familiar with them, as my husband and I had them in three of our last homes. We loved music and had a sound system in our homes that included the CD changers.

Her 5-CD changer was not working, and she bought a new one hoping I could replace the old one with the new one. The CD Changer was in a huge wall-to-wall unit with lots of electronics and lots of cords running down the wall behind the CD changer.

The cord on the back of the CD changer was hard wired to the unit so it could not be unplugged from there. I tried to follow the cord down, but there were too many cords running down several shelves making it difficult to follow.

I asked her what she planned to do with the old CD changer. She was going to get rid of it. I told her I would just cut the cord. She got me a pair of shears from the garage to cut the cord. At this point, I honestly don't know where my brain was, but I definitely was not thinking. Just as I started cutting into the cord, I heard a mental voice very loudly and sternly say, "Stop, there's electricity"! I stopped and realized my mistake.

I had already cut the cord but not enough to get electrocuted or to corrupt the cord. The end result was the CD changer was not the problem. The receiver that it was connected to had a little electrical "hiccup" which I resolved. We were able to wrap the cord of the old CD changer with electrical tape and set it back in service.

As I left her home, I "thanked" whoever gave me the stern warning.

Decision Help and Love Gift Message
November 12, 2015

Jewelry has not been important to me. When it came to gifts, Pete knew that he didn't need to worry about buying me jewelry. I loved my "techy" toys and preferred them to jewelry.

I had been struggling for months on whether to let my business go so that I could move forward with my life. I had many wonderful customers and loved my work, but the work was consuming me. I had no life beyond technology. I felt a need to move forward and explore new opportunities in life.

I missed having Pete to talk too especially regarding decisions. He was a wonderful sounding board for helping me think through things. On November 12, 2015, I was driving to lunch and having a conversation with Pete, as if he was sitting in the passenger seat of my car. I was sharing how I missed him and needed his help when I heard the words, "My mother calls me Alvin," which was his birth name. I kind of laughed at this thought and commented back, "Yes, your mother loved your name, Alvin, and called you Alvin." I continued my conversation with him only using his birth name, Alvin. He had acquired the nickname, Pete, when he was younger and it just stuck with him. He used the name Pete for everything but legal things. I met him as Pete.

When I got home after lunch and my afternoon appointments, I picked up my mail. There was a marketing card that so overwhelmed me, I had to stop and catch my breath. It was addressed to Alvin, my husband's birth name. In the 25 years that we were together, we never got mail from this company, and Pete never used his birth name when making purchases. He always used Pete.

It was the message that it conveyed that meant something to me, and I knew exactly what it meant. It read, "Alvin, have you told Stephanie just how much you love her?" There was a picture of a beautiful oval pendant that had my birth name, Stephanie, at the top with three hearts in the middle that said, "I Love You" in the hearts and his birth name, Alvin, in the bottom of the oval pendant.

What an amazing loving message and the timing? Coincidence? The way the day's events transpired clearly showed me positive confirmation to move forward with my decision to close my business, so that I could move forward with my life. Pete always had a unique way of getting my attention when it came to making decisions. I knew my heart had been heard, and I got the message. I knew what I needed to do.

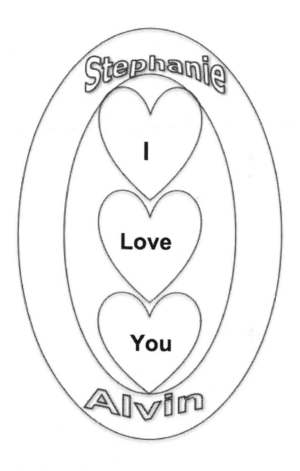

Pendent Illustration - November 12, 2015

Doorbell & Smoke Alarms
December 2015

December 2015 started out as a difficult month. I had made the decision to close my business, and I had written a letter to all my customers of my decision. I started scaling back my calendar appointments.

The morning of December 3, 2015, I had an emotional meltdown. I knew in my heart I had made the right decision, but I was stressing about it too. My practice of releasing stress was to dance. I love to dance and had taken up line dancing a few months earlier as a way to release stress and do something other than technology. It was around 10 in the morning, and I was dancing in my great room about two feet from the front door when the doorbell rang. I went to the door, but no one was there. I had this strange sensation though that someone was there.

On December 4, 2015, at 9:15 in the morning, the smoke alarm in my office beeped, just one time. The battery was fairly new so I didn't think it could be the battery. Again, I had this feeling that someone was near.

On December 8, 2015, at 9:30 in the morning, the doorbell rang again. I was in my office, which is about 15 feet from the front door. No one was there.

On December 11, 2015, at 1:30 in the afternoon, the doorbell rang and again around 7:30 in the evening. Both times no one was at the door. After the 7:30 pm doorbell ring, I went back into the kitchen, and there I smelled Pete's aftershave. I felt he was right in front of me and sensed he was showing me love and support for the decision I had made.

On December 20, 2015, around 5 in the evening, the doorbell rang and as you guessed no one was there. I wasn't ready to think there was something wrong with the doorbell yet because I just had this heightened awareness that I was not alone.

December 24, 2015, Christmas Eve, around 7:20 in the evening, the doorbell rang and as always no one was there. At 10 pm on Christmas Eve, the smoke detector in the master bedroom chirped just one chirp and no more. I again sensed Pete's presence by the essence of his aftershave. Sometime after midnight, I sensed my left hand being nudged. The twitching in my hand was weird. I felt like someone was holding my hand. It was Christmas morning.

On December 26, 2015, around 4 in the afternoon, the doorbell rang and no one was there. Now I found myself answering the door and welcoming whomever into the villa. Around 8 that night, the smoke detector in the master bedroom chirped one time.

After these December events there were no more. By the end of December my stress about closing my business had subsided. I was feeling calmer and happier about the decision.

My customers had received their letters and many of them fully understood and supported me. December 2015 ended up being the happiest holiday season since the passing of Pete. I felt totally surrounded by love.

2016

Messages

Unusual Encounter at Restaurant
January 8, 2016

It was about 2:30 in the afternoon on Friday, January 8, 2016, I went to a restaurant that I frequent to get a late lunch. I had just come from having a mammogram, and it had not gone well.

As I opened the door to go into the restaurant, a man was standing at the cash register, which is located just inside the front door. He whirled around and smiled at me, but this was no ordinary smile. His face literally twinkled. I remember thinking to myself in that instant that his face "twinkled." I could not help but stare because his face just radiated this light. I tried to look into his eyes, but because of this twinkling effect, I could not really see into his eyes.

I was embarrassed, as I realized I was staring. I went to the hostess station and was immediately signaled by one of the waitresses to sit wherever I wanted (which was normal because I frequent this restaurant). The restaurant was not busy at this time, so it was easy to get a good booth to look out over the beautiful water features and golf course. I went to a sidewall booth that allowed me to look out both the side and front windows. There was only one very large round booth in front of me, but it was empty. In fact, there was only one other couple in the entire restaurant.

I was playing Scrabble on my iPad. I looked up and this same man with the "twinkling" face was now sitting in the big round booth in front of me. He was lined up perfectly with me, but with his back to me. I was startled because to access the big corner booth in front of me, he had to either walk beside my booth or in front of me to sit in that booth. I don't know how I missed his coming or sitting in that booth in front of me. Then in my mind I was questioning, "Why would he sit in this over-sized booth directly in front of me when there are five more normal sized booths at the front windows and another four normal-sized booths behind me and almost all the tables in the restaurant are open?"

The waitress did not wait on him. It appeared that he was drinking a cup of coffee or something, and I saw a cellophane bag, which I assumed, was cookies. The restaurant was known for their baked goods.

I had this very strange feeling about this man, and I remember feeling as if he could read my mind. It was a little unsettling.

He finished his coffee or whatever he was drinking and got up to leave. I was hoping that as he got up out of that booth, I might have an opportunity to look into his eyes or see his face again. I wanted to see if his face really "twinkled."

When he got up out of the booth, he purposely turned and looked at me and smiled, and again his face just "twinkled." I think he said something to me, but I was so mesmerized by his face and trying so hard to look into his eyes, that I don't remember what he said; but it was purposeful on his part to specifically turn and look at me. I felt I knew him, and if I could just look into his eyes I would know, but I just could not see into his eyes.

I again realized I was staring. In my embarrassment, I looked down for a moment and when I looked up, he was walking away. It was at that moment that I recognized the familiarity. He walked like my Pete and had on khaki cargo pants just like Pete wore before he passed away. Khaki cargo pants or shorts were favorites of Pete's. This man also had on a jacket like Pete wore. Then the man was gone.

This incident shook me up. I was feeling so much emotion. Even though I didn't know what it meant, I did not want to forget it. I went home and wrote down everything I could remember.

The following day, Saturday, January 9, 2016, I decided to try a set of comforting cards that a friend had given me in 2014. I had not been comfortable with the idea of the cards when they were given to me, but from all that had been happening in the last couple of years, I decided to give them a try.

I followed the instructions for preparing the cards for use. I shuffled the cards and a card popped up which meant it was the card you should read. The message on the card that popped up for me read, "I watch over you every day." It was at that moment I felt I was given the answer to the unusual incident at the restaurant that occurred the day before.

The following Monday, I received a call telling me that my mammogram needed to be repeated. This news would usually have upset me, but I was more at peace. The incident of the "twinkling" face on the previous Friday and the comforting card on Saturday seemed to be making more sense. I felt a comfort that heaven was watching over me and that all would be just fine, and it was.

I have gone back to that restaurant many times around that same time and at other times hoping to see that man and his "twinkling" face again. I have never seen him again. His twinkling face and the whole nature of the encounter reminded me of another similar encounter that I had in the 90's that I didn't understand at the time but never forgot. Are these types of encounters heaven showing us love? I was starting to sense that heaven is around us all the time; we just need to be open and receptive to heaven's love and presence, and recognize the signs.

First Dream
May 5, 2016

I have had dreams all my life, but usually on waking the dream is gone. The dream I had on this occasion stayed with me upon waking and had a very loving effect on me.

I don't know the exact time on this dream, but I believe it was early morning. I was in that state between being asleep and awake when I felt a presence on my left side. When I turned my face to the left to see who was there, I saw Pete's face. He was younger looking but I can't say whether 30's or 40's but definitely younger than when he passed away. At that moment, the feeling that I have had about apiece in my heart missing was gone. My heart felt whole again. I remember saying in the dream, "You're home." My sense of life with Pete, for that instant, seemed as it was when he was alive.

When I woke up, the dream was crystal clear, and my left hand was positioned as if I was holding someone's hand. I know that it was only a dream, but upon waking I felt so loved. This was the beginning of several wonderful dreams over the next few months.

Message from Spirit
June 23, 2016

In 2015 I had attempted to sign up with an online dating service. As I was completing the application, I heard the words, "I am taking care of this." I stopped, as I was learning that it was best to pay attention to these unusual messages.

It was about a year later; June 23, 2016, and I was at the same restaurant where I had the unusual encounter with the man whose face "twinkled." I had just about finished my lunch when a woman approached me. I thought she might be a new employee as she was spending time with some of the waiters, but she was not dressed as a waiter. She was dressed in a nice skirt and blouse with a pearl necklace. She asked me if I was a Christian. I said, "Yes." She then proceeded to tell me that "spirit" wanted her to give me a message. I was a little shocked, as I have never had a "spirit" message before.

She told me that I had been praying about something and had recently given up on it. I knew immediately what that meant. The previous day I had again asked God for a companion. Later that same day I saw a posting for a senior dating service which I had not seen before, so I thought it might be a sign from God that it was okay to proceed. I signed up for a 30-day trial. I didn't feel or hear any message while I was applying that I was to wait, so I figured I was good.

This woman went on to tell me that spirit said, "Do not give up and wait for Him (meaning God), and that He had a blessing for me." In fact, she said, 'It was a double blessing, and it was just around the corner." She also said there would be a sign. She didn't understand the sign, but she said I would have a sign.

I was overwhelmed by this second unusual encounter at the same restaurant that I had the first unusual encounter with the man with the twinkling face just months before. This was also the second time God asked me to "wait."

I saw this woman again on July 9, 2016, and she shared another message with me. She said, "Even though it is now unseen, so it all ready is." She also shared with me that the sign would be the eyes. I did learn her name that day.

I have never had a "spirit" message before, but I knew the moment she gave me the first message exactly what I had done and what it meant. I am to wait. God's timing and corners are not quite the same as human timing and corners and not always what we desire. I know from experience though that God's way is best. So I wait.

Remember This
July 21-27, 2016

After my spirit messages from the woman at a local restaurant, I had more unusual encounters. It seems God works with me in three's. When something happens three times, there is usually meaning in it. This series of encounters had to do with the name or word "Mike."

The first encounter was while I was having a conversation with a local acquaintance named "Mike," and during our conversation I heard the mental words, "Remember this." I mentally reviewed our conversation and could not find any significant part of our conversation that would trigger those words. It seemed it was related to the word or name "Mike."

A couple days later I saw this same acquaintance named "Mike," and I heard the words "Remember this." Again, there was nothing in our conversation that related to the previous conversation or that seemed significant. I knew him and his wife from local gatherings. Outside of these two encounters, I had not heard these words "remember this" before in any previous conversations with him and/or his wife or anyone else.

A day later I was at a homeowner's event. I had picked a table close to the door, as I needed to slip away early. A man approached my table and asked if he could sit at the table. At that point, there was no one else sitting at the table. I said, "Of course," and he put a notebook down and left. When he returned he introduced himself as "Mike." Again I heard the mental words, "Remember this." I introduced myself and this "Mike" said his wife's name was the same as my name, "Lynn." Lynn is actually my middle name. I have gone by my middle name since first grade, which is another story. He introduced her when she arrived at the table. I was sitting there chuckling to myself at the three references to "Mike" in one week, and then this last one with his wife having the same name as myself.

At the time of this writing, I don't know what the reference to "Mike," means, but three times in one week and hearing the words, "remember this," I know it means something, and I will understand when the time is right.

God's Principle
on Obedience
September 27-28, 2016

In February of 2014, I had a personal visit from the Area Ambassador of a large Georgia TV church that Pete and I had supported. I had not had any further personal communication from the Area Ambassador since 2014 until September 27, 2016. He communicated with me via email. He again thanked me for partnering with his organization, and then gave me a Principle from another book by the pastor of this large Georgia church. The Principle was about Obedience and God's Blessing. The meaning of the Principle was basically to "wait on the Lord."

The next day, September 28, 2016, my daily devotion was on Obedience and "waiting on the Lord."

These two messages on Obedience within 24 hours left an impression on me. They reminded me of the "spirit" messages that I had received just a couple months earlier to wait, and the wait message from the previous year. It seemed as a loving, gentle reminder that heaven's timing and human timing are so different, and I was to wait on God and His blessings. I believe God was letting me know that He had not forgotten me.

Code from the Internet
November 19, 2016

Pete and I did silly things that made marriage fun. I had one silly thing that always made Pete roll his eyes and shake his head, but it made him smile. I loved to see him smile. Because he was a telephone man, when I had an empty toilet tissue roll, I would go through the house calling through the empty toilet roll, "Calling Sweetie Petey, Calling Sweetie Petey."

Even though he was no longer around, once in a while I still found myself calling him through the empty toilet tissue roll. I could imagine him rolling his eyes and shaking his head, but still the smile.

On the morning of November 19, 2016, I had gone through this little ritual with an empty toilet tissue roll. Later that morning I was online ordering tickets to a local concert. There was the usual screen asking for me to show I wasn't a robot, and I was to type in the code given to me. The code was YUCALPETE. I just starred at this. To me it read, "Why You Call Pete." I sensed he was letting me know that he heard me calling him. It made me smile after I got over the initial shock of seeing it.

Angel & Comfort
Dreams & Wind Kisses
December 2016

Even though several years have passed since I lost Pete, the holidays were still hard. December 9, 2016, I went to a Christmas concert at the church where Pete had worked for nine years. They loved him and always reminded me of their love. That evening the Director of the Choral group that gave the Christmas concert came up and introduced his wife, and then went on to talk about my Pete. It made my heart ache.

That night I had a dream. There was a very, very large angel approaching me. The angel was so large that it appeared as if the wall and ceiling of my bedroom were gone, and the angel consumed that whole area and on up into the sky. The angel was huge and had very large wings. In my dream I commented to the angel on how large he was, and somehow I knew who he was and called him by name, "Gabriel." There were other angels too but not as large. I don't remember receiving any message just this awesome huge presence. I felt love and peace in this dream with the presence of this huge heavenly angel and cast of angels.

I don't know if there was a relationship to the Christmas concert that I had attended the night of the dream. I only know that I felt love in the dream and upon waking.

On the following night, after my angel dream, I had another dream. Pete was comforting me. I was sitting on his lap the way I always did and he was comforting me. I don't know why he was comforting me: maybe because it was the holidays.

Around the same time of the dream of the angel Gabriel and of Pete, I started having another nighttime event.

At night in that state between being awake and asleep, I would have the strongest sensation that someone just blew air across my right cheek. Although it was soft, it was strong enough that it would startle me awake. The first couple of times I did not understand what I was experiencing, but as this phenomena continued, I started calling them my "wind kisses."

Although it was not every night, it was frequent. I felt very loved by these "wind kisses." Sometimes there would be more than one "wind kiss" which made me giggle or smile and I always said, "Thank you." I felt very loved. As of this writing, the "wind kisses" still happen.

Dream of Friend
December 29, 2016

In 2002 I was asked by a local senior church to network their computers. On my first day at the church, a member of the church came into the office and without any hesitation asked, "Who is this?" The Administrative Assistant told her that I was assisting them with their computers. The church member said, "I need you." Although she was 30 plus years older than me, it was the start of a long and beautiful friendship.

Sometime in our friendship she asked if I would create a memorial presentation for her celebration of life service. At the time, I chuckled as I thought she would probably outlive me. She had a vibrant active life. Her life was so vibrant and active that her son wrote a book about her life. This publication was mostly for family and friends. She gave me an autographed copy of her book.

Over the years, she would hand me photos that she wanted in the memorial presentation. I would take them home and scan them to my computer for the presentation. There were many photos from her 90 plus years of life, and she did have an active life. Some of the photos had notes on the back indicating the time frame and place but many did not have any notation.

I made small thumbnails of all the photos she supplied me, and numbered them, and made room for descriptions. We were going to work on identifying the photos together on one of my visits, but each visit she would have other things for us to do, so we never quite got to this identification of photos process.

Fast forward to 2016, and my friend was now in her mid-90's and was having some health issues. In November 2016, she asked if I would visit to help her send out her annual Christmas letter. This was an annual event for us. She still communicated with over 200 people either via email or US postal mail. Although she was computer literate, this task was too daunting for her to do alone.

I was scheduled for early December. My friend's health took a nosedive. She went into the hospital, so her husband was going to contact me when she got back home. When he did contact me, he said she would not be going back home, but was in hospice care. He told me that she still wanted her Christmas letter sent out. I had to smile; this was so typical of my friend. Always in control and knowing exactly what she wanted done. The Christmas letter was finished but needed to be set up to fit on Christmas stationery for mailing and also emailed. Her husband said he would do the printing and mailing if I would do the emailing.

I arranged to go on December 20, 2016. I met with her husband, and we finished the email to all her friends. I showed him the printer setup for the postal service mailings. We then walked over to the hospice unit so that I could visit with her. As we were walking over to the hospice unit, I asked her husband if he was aware of her request for me to do her memorial presentation. He was not aware of it. I told him about all the photos I had compiled over the years, and how we hadn't quite gotten to the point of identifying some of the photos so that I would know where they fit in her life events. I told him I would start working on the presentation and get it to them both soon to review.

On Thursday, December 29, 2016, while having lunch, I had this nagging sensation that I needed to finish the memorial presentation for my friend. I felt this nagging was coming from my friend. She was an extremely loving person, but very much in control. I went home after lunch and started working on her memorial presentation.

I was stuck with the photos that I could not identify, when I felt the nudging to get the book my friend's son had written about her life. I got the book and started going through it, and sure enough some of the photos in the book were photos that I had but didn't know where they fit. Through the book on her life, I was able to identify all the photos but one. Her daughter identified that last photo later.

That Thursday, December 29, 2016, around 8:30 pm, I emailed a copy of the presentation to my friend in hospice. I knew she had her iPad with her in hospice. She was still alert and sharp as a tack when I saw her a few days before. In the email I asked her if she could review the presentation and let me know if it was close to what she wanted. I also sent a copy to her husband.

I was exhausted, as I had stayed with this project from lunch through 8:30 pm. I went to bed. That night I had a dream about my friend. She was trying to give me a name. She kept telling me the name, and the last name was so unusual that I remember asking, in the dream, if she would spell the last name for me. Just as I asked her to spell the last name, I woke up. The dream was so vivid I wrote it down. I was sure the name she gave me in the dream had something to do with her memorial presentation.

That morning, Friday, December 30, 2016, I had an email from her husband that my friend had passed away at 9:30 pm the previous night, December 29, 2016. This was just an hour after I sent the memorial presentation to them both. Although, I doubted that she physically saw the presentation, I sensed that she knew it was done. I felt that I had gotten it right.

I asked her husband and family if they understood the meaning of the name from the dream. They did not know what the name meant, but because of her many life affiliations, they too felt it might have been someone in her life.

To this day I have no idea what the name given to me in the dream means. Maybe I will know some day. The name did have "Michael" in it.

2017

Dreams

Dream of Missie
March 1, 2017

At Christmas in 1974, I was given a puppy as a present. I was not able to have children, so my husband at that time and my sisters decided a puppy would be good for me. The puppy they selected for me, as I understand it, was a renegade from the rest of the litter. My family decided that this renegade puppy was the one for me.

I named my little renegade puppy "Missie" because she "missed" the whole idea of doggie potty training. Every method imaginable was used to try to help her understand the concept of letting us know when she needed to go outside or while outside what she was supposed to do. We tried the smelly papers concept and that only caused her to smell the papers with her nose but with her backside off the papers; only to pee on the floor. She was the funniest, most loving furry friend I ever had, but she wasn't too bright. It took almost two years to potty train her, but she finally got it.

Early in Missie's life we also tried dog training school. At the first lesson, she would not focus on the training, so they asked me to leave and come back in an hour. When I returned, I could hear all this laughter inside. The trainers said to me, "She is adorable and funny, but don't bother bringing her back." She just didn't get that either.

Throughout the 15 years that I had this wonderful renegade, she provided me with so much love, joy and laughter. I do believe dogs have spirits, and that they understand our emotions and our needs. They give so much of themselves to their owners, and my Missie gave me her all.

I lost my beloved Missie in June 1989 to cancer. Her choker and tags have been draped around the neck of a stuffed dog given to me by a very special couple. They loved Missie, and the stuffed dog resembled Missie. After she was gone, occasionally I would think I heard her tags jingle, like they did when she would shake her head to make them jingle to get my attention, especially at night. I had not heard the jingle in a long time.

On the night of March 1, 2017, I had a dream about Missie. I had not thought about her in years, but that night she was as real as if she were right there doing her normal thing when she wanted my attention.

In my dream, I was sleeping and was awakened by her shaking her head to get those tags to jingle to get my attention. She wanted to go outside. I remember saying to her in the dream, "I don't remember if I fed you. I don't even have a water dish out for you." It was like I knew I didn't have her anymore, but there she was, and I was feeling guilty for not having a water dish for her or even remembering if I fed her. Then I woke up.

The dream was so real; I honestly expected to see her by my bed when I woke up. The little stuffed dog with Missie's choker and tags have been draped on a chair near my bed for some time. I had a very warm and happy feeling that morning. I felt like I had a furry hug from heaven.

Pete in Funny Dream and Unusual Email
April 18, 2017

Pete and I were runners. I always loved running in the rain but not in thunderstorms. When there was lightning around, the hair on my arms would stand up, and I just preferred not to be anywhere close to the source. Pete and I had been caught in thunderstorms several times when running. We would take shelter where we could and that sometimes included the cove of garage doors.

On Tuesday, April 18, 2017, I had a dream of a man that looked to be in his 30's or 40's. He had on a trench coat and it was raining. In this dream, I had been running and had taken shelter from the rain inside the small cove of somebody's garage door. The man in the trench coat approached me. He asked for a drink. At that point in the dream, I realize that I have an orange drink in my hand. I gave him my orange drink, and he kept drinking it and stepping in closer to me. I was uncomfortable with his closeness, and he was drinking all my drink. I told him he was a little too close and asked if he was going to drink all my drink. He took the drink away from his mouth and smiled. At that moment in the dream, I knew it was my Pete and I said, "Oh, it's you Pete!" Then I woke up. It was 4:53 in the morning. The behavior of the man in the trench coat in the dream was so like that of Pete. He loved teasing me. Even though I don't remember a storm in the dream, the shelter was something that was real in thunderstorms, and the silliness of the closeness was so like Pete.

The same morning of the dream, I received the second strange email on my iPhone similar to one I had received in January 2017. I wrote about the first one in my journal but I could not find any relevance regarding it except that it was a fluke. This second one was similar to the first one. There was "No Sender," "No Message Content," "No Subject," and dated 12/31/69. I knew it would disappear just like the first one as soon as I scrolled through the email, so I took a screen shot so that I could study it later.

Although. I learned there was documentation on these types of emails, in all the years I have been doing technology, which included thousands of training and troubleshooting emails; I had never, ever received this type of email before. Now in a short period of time, I had received two. The first one I received just a couple of months earlier, but I ignored it. I share this email event only because of the timing of it with the dream I had the night before. I am learning that nothing is a coincidence; there is meaning in all events and especially the timing of events.

I had this wonderful feeling that it was Pete letting me know he was still watching over me and having fun at it. He was also a young Pete in the dream just as the medium had said in her reading for my stepdaughter in 2014!

●   4:38 AM ›

Discover 24 ways to transform your health
If you are unable to see the message below, click
here to view. This email is brought to you by

●   4:31 AM ›

Amazing Men's Spring Deals + Free Shipping

● **No Sender**   12/31/69 ›
No Subject
This message has no content.

●   4:07 AM ›

Join   and Discover The   Secrets of...
If you are unable to see the message below, click
here to view. This email is brought to you by Gre...

●   3:47 AM ›

Preview summer with 25% off & free shipping.
This message has no content.

●   3:33 AM ›

You have a new electronic   Summary N...
You have a new electronic   Summary
Notice (   ) ready in your account. Follow the...

●   3:31 AM ›

Dad and Unusual Email
May 9, 2017

I was worried about my dad, and during my prayer time I asked for help for him. He was 90 and would be undergoing carotid surgery. There was a risk of stroke especially at his age. At that time both my parents lived with my sister in a lovely casita on her property. Dad did a lot of caregiving for my mom, who had dementia, so a stroke would create a difficult situation.

That morning when I opened my email on my iPhone, I had the third email that was like the previous two from January and April. It was Grey with "No Sender" and "This message has no content." This one was dated 12/31/00 and "No Subject" was missing. Knowing that the message would disappear the moment I scrolled through the email, I did another screen shot of the message as I did the one on 4/18/2017. As soon as I scrolled, it was gone just like the previous two strange emails.

Even though there is documentation on these types of emails, it is the timing of them. This was the third one since January, and this one was received after I had lifted my dad up in prayer. I had this lovely feeling again that my prayer for my dad was heard.

At the time of writing this book, I have not received anymore of these strange emails. The fact that I received three in a short period of time usually has meaning for me. God seems to deal with me in three's. The first strange email may have been just to get me tuned in to what was coming. The second two followed very specific events, and I had a peaceful feeling that I was loved and heard.

Dream of Heaven
July 5, 2017

The year 2017 seemed to be the year of dreams for me. I have had more dreams that I remember on waking then I can recall from my past.

In this dream on July 5, 2017, I saw the heavens open above me and a very bright light was shining on me. It was as if I my ceiling had opened to the heavens, and there was this bright-white warm light. The sky was a blue that I have never seen before, and there were these beautiful puffy white clouds. The clouds were not like any clouds that I have ever seen. They were perfectly shaped clouds. It was serene and beautiful. I didn't want it to go. Then I woke up. I felt so much peace and love in this dream. It was like the love that I have felt on those occasions when I have experienced what I called my "God hugs."

To this day, I have no idea what the dream means. It was beautiful, loving and peaceful beyond words. If this was a glimpse of heaven, I can only say, "Oh wow!"

Mike - More References
July 15, 2017 and September 5, 2017

A year earlier, in July of 2016, I was told to remember the word or name "Mike" three times during the week of July 21-27, 2016. I wrote each one of the references in my journal although I didn't understand their meaning.

Then the night my dear friend passed away in December 2016, I had a dream that she kept trying to tell me a name, which included the name "Michael."

On Saturday, July 15, 2017, I received a phone call, which I did not answer because the number was unknown to me, and I was having lunch. I knew a message would be left if the caller wanted to be known. The caller did leave a message. Before I had the chance to listen to the first message another call came in from that same number. Then I had two voicemail messages.

The first voicemail message was from a woman from our Community Fitness Center. She called to tell me that my paint class had been cancelled. My phone also transcribes the voicemail messages so that I can visually read the messages. The transcribed message was the same as the voice message.

The second voicemail message was again from the same woman from the Fitness Center saying that she forgot to tell me to pick up my check. However, the transcription of this message was, "This is "Mike" from the Fitness Center calling, etc." I had to laugh. The woman from the fitness center had a name staring with a "P" and it was nowhere close to the sound or name "Mike." It gave me a smile and seemed to be a gentle reminder that the name or word "Mike" still meant something.

On September 5, 2017, I had another reference to the name or word Mike. That morning during prayer time, I asked God if the word or name "Mike" still meant something. I had so many references to the name or word "Mike," but nothing was materializing to help me know what all these references meant.

That afternoon I received a phone call from an unknown number from northern Arizona. The caller left me a message.

When I listened to the message, the caller said his name was "Mike." I immediately had the impression to "remember this." This particular Mike was calling for someone named Bob. The call seemed important, so I texted Mike back to let him know that the number he called did not have a Bob connected to it. Mike texted me back. I learned that his last name was the same as my maiden name and spelled exactly the same way. I had a strong sensation that I was to "remember this" again. I don't believe in coincidences. I had just asked God that morning if the word or name "Mike" was still important.

God has given me quite a few signs regarding the word or name "Mike," so I know it must mean something, and I will know what it means when heaven is ready for me to know.

Love Note in the Mail
August 8, 2017

The summer of 2017 I felt God telling me He wasn't done with me yet, and that He wanted me to share the love He had shown me. It became apparent that He wanted me to share my journal. I was not comfortable with the sharing idea or comfortable that I was a writer. God gently reminded me that this was His love story, and that I had been writing all my adult life.

On the morning of August 8, 2017, my spirits were a little low. I sometimes go days without a lot of human interaction and hugs. During my prayer and meditation time that morning, I asked for a love sign. I knew that I was loved, but I am human and sometimes I just need to hear or feel loved.

When I am feeling a little down, I know it is a sign that I need to get out of the house and go do something preferably with someone. I had contacted a friend about lunch but did not hear back from her, so I went to lunch alone and did some window-shopping.

That afternoon when I got home and got my mail, there was another marketing card from the same company that sent one almost two years earlier. This one was addressed to my first name, Stephanie, which was unusual. Since first grade I have been known to everyone but family by my middle name,

Lynn. This marketing card had a picture of a beautiful oval pendant that read,

> "Stephanie,
> I loved you then,
> I love you still,
> I always have,
> I always will.
> Alvin."

I just stood there stunned and in tears, but they were happy tears.

As I was writing in my journal about this special mailing and the message, I realized it was the anniversary of Pete and I meeting back in 1988 and going on our first date, which was a run together. I asked for a love sign in that morning's prayer and "wow" did I get one. It may not have been a physical human hug, but what a powerful love message and hug from heaven.

June 2018: Update to this chapter. The time had come to turn over this book to the publisher. I was having the same anxiety about sharing my journal as I did back in the summer of 2017 when God initially nudged me to share this journal of His love.

Saturday morning, June 23, 2018, as I was running, I mentally mentioned my anxiety and asked if I was doing the right thing. I asked for a sign. I barely finished that mental thought when I saw the twinkles in the sky. I have seen them before on occasions. It was daybreak; there were no stars, but I was seeing this twinkling in the sky. It made me smile and gave me goose bumps; I felt encouraged. When I got home and stretched on my stretching rock, I had a hummingbird fly up to me on my left and it hovered within a foot of me. It then sat on a tree branch in front of me and turned so that it was making direct eye contact with me. We just stared at each other. Then it came fluttering back in front of me and both times I thought it was going to land on my outstretched hand. It flew and sat again on a branch right in front of me and turned so that we had eye contact. It stayed like this until I broke the eye contact. Then it flew off. I felt the strangest energy, and I knew in my heart that I was given amazing signs of positive encouragement to proceed with this book.

It doesn't end there. That night, Saturday, June 23, 2018, I was awakened and led to write down these words. "The marketing card and message you received were not only about the anniversary of meeting Pete, but also a message of love and encouragement to do as you were asked to do." I did not see this revelation at the time that I received this second marketing card back in August 2017! I only connected it with the anniversary of meeting Pete.

Wow!

Dream of Trees

November 7, 2017

This dream was different than the other dreams. It did not involve people only trees.

It was a dream of two trees and their love for a smaller broken branch. The two trees were on the left. It was almost as if I were looking at a picture of trees that are at the left edge of the picture. There was an upper tree and a lower tree. The leaves of the two trees were a vibrant rich green, and the branches were beautiful shades of browns. I could not see the trunks of the trees in my dream only the upper branches with leaves.

In this dream the wind was blowing really hard from the left to the right, and the branches on both trees appeared to be really leaning and extended to the right as if they were reaching out. Then I saw a small tree branch on the right that seemed to be trying to reach the upper tree, but the wind kept it from reaching the upper tree. All of a sudden, the bottom tree's branches swept up and cradled and lifted the little branch so that it could reach the upper tree's branches. In the dream, the little tree branch's leaves appeared to kiss the upper tree as it reached it, and the upper tree looked as if it was hugging the little tree branch. Then I woke up.

It was a beautiful dream and although I didn't know what it meant, I knew that heaven would show me the meaning in time. The colors were so vibrant; there just aren't words to adequately describe the colors. It made me wonder if heaven is this colorful.

Trees
November 17, 2017

In 2014 when I moved into a lovely villa in a new community, there was a very large Sissoo tree in the front yard. When I had my pre-owner home inspection, the home inspector showed me how this lovely Sissoo tree was lifting up my front sidewalk. I loved the tree, and I wasn't going to ask the owner to fix it, which might kill the tree. He wrote it up, but I did nothing.

We had a lot of rain for Arizona, and the tree grew exponentially as did the root under the sidewalk to my front door. I already had several people trip on the uplifted side walk. In 2015 I had the tree topped and cropped way back to slow the growth, but that only seemed to help the tree grow faster and taller.

In 2016 my community banned the Sissoo trees, but allowed those who had them to keep them. Several neighbors decided to remove their Sissoo trees, and I decided to have my two Sissoo trees removed too. The front yard Sissoo was cut down, and the main trunk was ground down to one foot underground. The left over underground trunk was painted with a stump killer. This was to deter Sissoo tree suckers from growing. Sissoo trees are notorious for large underground root systems and when the trees are removed, those remaining root systems try to grow new trees. These new growths are called "suckers." It can take up to three years to kill off all the root system of a Sissoo tree if the tree is not removed carefully.

Sissoo trees are also known to kill other new trees that might grow near where they have been removed. My landscaper felt we should wait before planting another tree. We waited almost a year until late February 2017 to plant a new tree. That gave me time to have the uplifted sidewalk replaced.

When the landscaper planted the new tree, he removed what he could of the remaining Sissoo tree trunk and any remaining root system to try to deter more suckers. He planted the new tree a few feet away from where the old Sissoo tree had been.

About a month after it was planted, we had a heat spell, and my new tree died. The landscaper thought it was just in shock from the heat wave. The weather returned to normal, and it did make a comeback and grew new leaves. Then our summer heat hit, and we had a very hot, dry summer in 2017. The tree died again by the end of June, and this time it didn't recover.

The landscaper was concerned about planting another tree, as he still felt that whatever was left of the old Sissoo tree might just kill another tree. Our front yards are small so there was not a lot of available space for planting a tree, and the community required one tree in the front yard.

By the time the summer heat left us, winter was just around the corner. I figured it would be spring 2018 before I had another new tree. Each day when I opened my front shutters, I would see my little dead tree and just sigh.

On the morning of Friday, November 17, 2017, I opened the front shutters as normal, and in my mind I thought, "Wouldn't it be nice to have a new tree for the holidays." I don't know why I thought this thought, but it just crossed my mind.

I went out for my morning run. I was gone about 50 minutes. When I came home, I almost thought I was at the wrong villa. There was a new tree, and it was stronger and actually prettier than the first one. I felt so much joy. I thanked "God" for hearing my random heart-felt thought that morning. I called my landscaper and "thanked" him for my new tree. I felt hugged from heaven, and I had a lovely tree for the holidays.

As I was writing this journal entry, I was reminded of the dream I had just 10 days earlier about the trees and the broken branch. Coincidence? I don't think so. I do believe all things happen for a reason, but in all honesty, I have not connected the dots between the dream of the trees and my new tree.

Ending Message

I end my story at the close of 2017, but the hugs, the love, and the help from heaven continue. Since my journey started in 2012, I have learned that heaven is more personal and interactive with us than I ever imagined. Even though I am by myself at this time in my life, which is different for me, I know that I am not alone, and that I am surrounded by heavenly love. I needed hugs and love, and heaven has sure provided.

When I wrote my journal entries, I only saw the one event as it happened. I wrote so that I would not forget these loving events and signs. I had no intention of sharing them, but God had other plans. In compiling my journal entries into this book, I realized that heavenly love was not just the past few years that I have been writing about, but have been showering down on me all my life. Past events that left an imprint on me, I now understand a little more fully what they meant and how heavenly love was surrounding me at that time. There are elements that I am still waiting on understanding, such as the reference to the word or name "Mike," and the messages of "waiting." I know that I will understand someday.

I also never thought about God allowing our loved ones, who have passed on before us, to continue to love, comfort, and help us as we continue on our life journey. I still don't know what happened in the summer of 2012 that turned on my sensitivities to receiving heavenly love and messages. I only know that I am more tuned into them now. I am amazed at the ways God works to get our attention. He will use whatever it takes to get His message across and shower us with heavenly love. Nothing is impossible with God even when it seems impossible to us.

My hope in sharing my journey is that others may come to know the hugs and love heaven has been bestowing on them. Heaven's love is around us all. We only need to listen with our hearts and not let our heads get in the way. Heavenly love will show up in many forms, as heaven is not limited in how hugs and love, or even humor and fun, are given.

May you feel and know heaven's presence and love ~

Stephanie Lynn Funk

Printed in the United States
By Bookmasters